MUSIC HALL MEMORIES

JACK HOUSE, Hon. LLD, doyen of Glasgow journalists, celebrated his eightieth birthday in May 1986. In his life as a working journalist, he has been a general reporter, features editor, crime reporter, local historian of Glasgow, film critic, book reviewer, writer on food and wine, and for 56 years theatre critic. It is in this last capacity that in his 54th book he looks back on seventy years of watching and listening to entertainment in the great Scottish tradition.

Here are innumerable and memorable anecdotes, character sketches and personal reminiscences of the great entertainers — including Sir Harry Lauder, Will Fyffe, Tommy Lorne, Dave Willis, Harry Gordon, Alec Finlay, Coco the Clown, George West, Tommy Morgan, G.S. Melvin —, and also of many others who achieved success or notoriety, all told with characteristic wit and affection. This is also a unique and fascinating record of artists and occasions on the stage and of the theatres themselves. Not the least engaging parts of the book are those in which Jack House describes his personal experiences as actor, radio comic, TV personality, circus clown and lion tamer!

Illustrated with historic photographs.

JACK HOUSE
—
MUSIC
HALL
MEMORIES

RICHARD DREW PUBLISHING
GLASGOW

First published 1986 by
Richard Drew Publishing Ltd
6 Clairmont Gardens
Glasgow G3 7LW

Editor Antony Kamm
Designed by James W Murray
The publisher is especially grateful to the following for
tracing photographs and arranging for the supply of prints:
William Doig; Joe Fisher; Jimmy Logan; Janet McBain;
Elizabeth Watson.

Set in Horley Old Style Semi Bold by John Swain (Glasgow) Ltd
Printed and bound in Great Britain by Cox and Wyman Ltd

ISBN 0 86267 167 1

PROGRAMME

—

THE
START
OF
IT ALL

IT SOUNDS IRISH, BUT music hall performances were taking place in Glasgow nearly a hundred years before there were any music halls in the city. The first star was a performing flea.

In the Glasgow Journal of 4 August 1763, there is an advertisement.

THIS IS TO ACQUAINT THE CURIOUS, That there is to be exhibited by the inventor and maker, S. Boverick, from nine in the morning till eight in the evening, at the sign of the Mason's Arms, opposite the Main Guard, Trongate, at one shilling each person, the so much admired collection of Miniature Curiosities, consisting of the following pieces:

1. An ivory chaise with four wheels, and all the proper apparatus belonging to them, turning readily on their axis together, with a man sitting on the chaise, all drawn by a flea, without any seeming difficulty, the chaiseman and flea being barely equal to a single grain.

2. A flea chained to a chain of 200 links, with a padlock and key — all weighing less than one-third of a grain. The padlock locks and unlocks. These two pieces are mentioned, with admiration, by Mr Henry Baker, of the Royal Society, in his book called 'Microscope made Easy', which the inventor and maker has by him, to show if required.

3. A landau, which opens and shuts by springs, hanging on braces, with four persons therein, two footmen behind, a

coachman on the box, with a dog between his legs, six horses and a postilion, all drawn by a single flea!

4. A pair of steel scissors weighing but the sixteenth part of a grain, which will cut a large horse-hair.

5. Thirty-six dozen of well-fashioned silver spoons in a pepper corn, and still room for several dozens more.

N.B. — The above curiosities have been shown to the Courts of England, France and Holland, the Royal Society in London, the Professors of Mathematics at Leyden, who have done the maker the honour to give testimonies of their approbation under their hands, in Latin, and nether Dutch, which may be seen by any person who desires it.

To be exhibited here no longer than the 13th inst., August.

Owners of flea circuses are always known as Professor and it would seem that Mr Boverick was a most accomplished miniaturist and deserved that title. The whole art of the flea circus is to make the equipment. One flea does all the tricks, for the simple reason that it is trying to escape. I saw a flea circus in an old building in Stockwell Street (so old that it was demolished years ago) and the Professor there had a flea which juggled a gold ball on its feet.

I was so impressed that I suggested to Andrew Stewart, then head of Light Entertainment for 5SC, the BBC radio station in Glasgow, that I might do a broadcast from the flea circus. Listeners, to be sure, wouldn't hear the flea, but they would hear the Professor in full flight with a running commentary by me on what the flea was doing. Unfortunately, by the time the BBC panjandrums in Blythswood Square had decided it was a good idea, the Professor and his flea had left Glasgow.

According to 'Senex', the principal contributor to that wonderful book, *Glasgow Past and Present,* a country wife from Pollokshaws was in Glasgow selling her fowls and eggs at the time of Boverick's demonstration. She did very well and so, on her way home, when she saw people crowding into the doorway where the sign of the Mason's Arms hung, paid her shilling without knowing what she was about to see, and arrived in the room just as the flea was drawing the ivory coach. All she noticed was the flea and she immediately put her thumb nail on it and cracked it, exclaiming 'Filthy beast, wha could hae brought you here?'

Professor Boverick went mad and seized the woman by the throat, demanding how she dared to kill his flea. 'Losh me, man,' said the wifie, 'makin' sic a wark about a flea. Gif you come wi' me to the Shaws, we'll gi'e ye a peck o' them and be muckle obliged to you for takin' them.' She would have been one of the original Queer Folk o' the Shaws. This story of the killing of the Professor's flea has been told ever since there were flea circuses but, for all we know, it may have happened in Glasgow first.

The Professor must have been very fond of his flea, for he fed it from his own arms and at night kept it snugly in a little box lined with soft velvet and silken ribbon, 'by which attentions,' says 'Senex', 'it came to be on friendly and intimate terms with its master'.

The flea was followed by the learned little horse from Courland, several learned dogs and Mr Nicholson's Learned Pig. Mr Nicholson appeared in Mr Frazer's Dancing Hall in King Street, near Glasgow Cross, and his pig could perform any of the tricks which the learned horse and dogs could do. The Glasgow Mercury mentioned that Mr Nicholson had in his lifetime 'taught a tortoise to fetch and carry articles at his pleasure; his overcoming the timidity of a hare by making her beat a drum; his perfecting six turkeycocks in a regular country dance; his completing a small bird in the performance of many surprising feats; his having taught three cats to strike several tunes on the dulcimer with their paws, and to imitate the Italian manner of singing.'

I don't know what the RSPCA would have said about that. But Jimmy Tarbuck, in his book, *Tarbuck on Showbiz*, reveals that a quarter of a century ago he appeared in a minor music hall with a chap who had a troupe of ducks which danced the cancan on the top of his piano. The secret was a hotplate built into the piano!

In Glasgow in the 18th century, the performing animals were followed by a succession of giants and dwarfs, and then came what you might call the first full music hall performance in the city. It was given in 'Mr Heron's great room in the Black Bull Inn, elegantly illuminated, warm and commodiously prepared'. The Black Bull in the Trongate was one of the finest taverns in Glasgow and Robert Burns always stayed there when he was in the city.

The entertainment was presented by a Prussian magician named simply Mr Breslaw. No one in Glasgow had seen a conjurer of his calibre. In the great room at the Black Bull the programme was as follows.

> 1st, Several select pieces of Music; the First Violin by a Foreign Young Lady, and Whistling the Notes by Sieur Arcalini.
> 2d, A Variety of Deceptions, quite new, by Mr BRESLAW, the particulars of which are expressed in the Bills.
> 3d, A Solo on the Violin by Miss Florella, who has had the

honour lately of performing before their Majesties and the Royal Family; and several Magical Card Deceptions by Sieur Andrea.

4th, Several new experiments on Watches, Silver Medals, Small Chests, Gold Boxes, Caskets, Silver Machineries, etc., etc., by Mr BRESLAW.

5th, The imitation of various Birds, by the New Venetian Rosignole, lately arrived from Naples.

The whole to conclude with a New Invented Silver Cup, and more than Fifty other Deceptions too numerous to insert.

That could have been a typical music hall programme if there had been any official music halls at the time. There were, however, theatres of a sort at Glasgow Green. The 'legitimate' theatres were in Dunlop Street and Queen Street and they had no connection with the music hall until music hall performers infiltrated the traditional pantomimes. Down on Glasgow Green, and especially at the foot of the Saltmarket were 'theatres' of various sizes, all built of wood and, sooner or later, going on fire. The poor relations were the penny geggies, which were often portable affairs and travelled Scotland when they were not on the Green. Geggie comes from an old Scots word, 'gegg', meaning a show.

Mumford's Penny Geggy was typical. Mr Mumford was one of those larger-than-life actors and liked his dram. There was the occasion when he was packing them in with Glasgow's favourite piece, *Rob Roy*. Mr Mumford was, naturally, the eponymous character. He got more and more incoherent as the play proceeded and eventually made an entrance with his red whiskers round one of his ears instead of his chin. Someone in the audience shouted, 'You're drunk!' Mr Mumford peered indignantly in the direction the voice came from. '*Me* drunk?' he cried. 'Wait till you see Bailie Nicol Jarvie!'

This has become a favourite theatrical story and has been told of most actors who imbibe too freely. Mumford was in the habit of appearing sometimes to do his spiel at the geggy entrance sufficiently sozzled to give the onlookers he was supposed to be attracting into the show a temperance lecture. He used himself as a bad example.

Some of the geggy actors also appeared in music hall-type shows. One was Johnnie Parry, an acrobat who was famous for 'the deid man's drap'. It could be introduced into almost any geggy show which included sudden death. A 'mountain' would be built

Glasgow Fair, *c.* 1825. (MITCHELL LIBRARY, GLASGOW)

Mumford's musicians. (MITCHELL LIBRARY, GLASGOW)

11

on the stage and, according to the plot, a character in the play was pursued up this mountain and shot. Johnnie Parry always played the fugitive. He would scramble to the top of the mountain and at that moment the fatal shot would ring out. Johnnie staggered about for a while and then did a spectacular slow fall down the mountainside.

He had a gift for relaxing, which meant the body which bounced and slid down the mountain looked like a dead one. Invariably this was received with ecstatic applause from the geggy audiences, with cries for an encore. After taking several bows, Johnnie would resume his original position on the stage and do the climb and fall all over again, after which, still to great applause, he would retire modestly into as much of the 'wings' as the geggy could afford.

On one occasion the applause and the shouting were so great that the geggy owner, afraid of a riot, asked Johnnie Parry to do the deid man's drap a third time. Johnnie obediently went through his routine once more and the audience again went mad. They fell silent as he reappeared, this time with a brush, with which he swept the whelk shells off the stage. The audience roared with laughter this time and the situation was saved.

In 1849 came the first brick theatre on Glasgow Green and *Glasgow, Past and Present* comments, 'Calvert, of the wooden Hibernian Theatre, obtained authority to erect a new brick edifice in Greendyke Street, immediately to the east of the Episcopal Chapel and adjoining the Model Lodging-Houses for the working classes. Now that the Adelphi Theatre, the City Theatre, and Cooke's Circus have all been swept off the Green by fire in less than four years, we have no doubt that this Hibernian will have 'ample room and verge enough' for dishing up the penny drama for the delectation and improvements of the canaille and young Red Republicans of the Bridgegate, the Wynds, Saltmarket, High Street, the Vennels, and the Havannah.'

The places mentioned were the worst slums of Glasgow in those days, and the comment reflects the Calvinistic attitude of many of the people in power in the city.

The first real music halls were starting in Glasgow at this same time. They had hardly a better reputation than the geggies, although they attracted what were then known as 'young swells' who wanted an unusual night out. They were mainly pubs with a stage, so that the audience might be eating and drinking while the acts performed. Possibly the nearest approach to them today are the clubs which, I hasten to say, are much better run than the first Glasgow music halls. There was one in Sauchiehall Street which was forced to erect a barrier between the audience and the performers because of the tendency of the gentlemen to try to get on to the stage to make the better acquaintance of the ladies appearing there.

One very popular place was Sloan's Oddfellows Music Hall in Argyle Street. The chairman there was James Bayliss and he was to become an important man in the history of the theatre in Glasgow. He and his wife had come from England and settled down in the city. Bayliss was ambitious and he was eventually able to take over the Milton Rooms at the top of Hope Street. He transformed the rooms into the Magnet Music Hall and put on a standard of performance that was much higher than some of its predecessors.

Alas, the Magnet went the way of most theatres in Glasgow. It was burned down. This, perhaps, was a blessing in disguise. James Bayliss built a new theatre, the Scotia Music Hall in Stockwell Street. All the leading lights of the London music hall appeared there, including Dan Leno, George Leybourne ('Champagne Charlie is me name'), Little Tich, Marie Lloyd, Harry Lauder (when he was unknown) and Charlie Coborn, who sang the two great hits of the time, 'Two Lovely Black Eyes' and 'The Man Who Broke the Bank at Monte Carlo'. Everybody thought he was the typical Cockney comedian, but his real name was Charles Whitton McCallum and he came from Argyll.

The reason he appeared as a Cockney was that Scotch comics were unpopular in London, though Irish comedians were lauded. London audiences said they couldn't understand Scotch. So Charles Whitton McCallum remained a Cockney comedian to the end of his performing days and never revealed to anyone that his son, Major David McCallum, was the Member of Parliament for Argyll.

Bayliss made a great success of the Scotia and went on to higher things. He opened his Royal Colosseum Theatre and Opera House in the Cowcaddens, not far from the Magnet. But perhaps he had not as sure a hand with the 'legit' and with opera, for he sold out to Glover and Francis and in 1869 the name was changed to the Theatre Royal. It was burned down, too.

The Scotia Music Hall continued on its winning way and was only challenged by the Royal Music Hall in Dunlop Street, just off Argyle Street. It was started by a wine-and-spirit merchant named David Brown. The Royal was praised highly by a popular Glasgow magazine, the Bailie, in 1873, which said that David Brown's name and music hall had been familiar in the city for at least a generation. Mr Brown gave up the Royal Music Hall in 1880, when it was renamed the Folly Music Hall by the new proprietors. That name lasted only one year, which is perhaps not surprising, and then it reverted to the original Royal. Without David Brown's touch it apparently lost its appeal and it finished up as an extension to a restaurant in the same building.

The Scotia's second rival was the Britannia Music Hall in the Trongate. It had been Campbell's Music Saloon but was considerably altered and enlarged by its new proprietors, A.M. Hubner and H.J. Rossborough. When a new owner changed the name to the Britannia Variety Theatre, he didn't worry about fact but described it as 'The Oldest Established Place of Amusement in Glasgow'. As far as is known, the Scotia made no protest.

By this time James Bayliss had died and the Scotia was taken over by his widow, who turned out to be every bit as enterprising as her husband. Indeed, if anything, she was the stronger personality. There was the case of the Lion Comique from London who died the death, as they say, on his first appearance at the Scotia. He flounced off the stage and went immediately to Mrs Bayliss's office. There he announced that he was leaving Glasgow that very night and would never darken the doors of the Scotia again.

Mrs Bayliss heard him out calmly. Then she produced his contract and said she would sue him if he didn't carry it out. The deflated Lion Comique had to work out his full week and was booed off the stage every night.

In the Harry Lauder legend there is a story of his first professional appearance — at the Scotia, of course. Harry was young and was determined he would not go back to the mines. Perhaps he tried too hard on the stage, but he did not disgrace himself. On Saturday he went to collect his week's salary. As she handed it over to him, Mrs Bayliss said to Lauder in a kind voice, 'There ye are, laddie. Noo awa' hame an' practise.'

This is a very nice story and it has been repeated for years. But Tom Colquhoun, a Glasgow theatre man in his own right and a nephew of Mrs Bayliss, pointed out to me that the 'old lady' spoke with a very English accent indeed and would have been quite incapable of saying 'Awa' hame an' practise.' There's no doubt, however, that Harry Lauder did practise — and to some tune!

TWO

LIFE BEFORE LAUDER

Harry Lauder was such a giant on the music hall stage that many people think the whole jingbang started with him. But, as I have demonstrated already, there was life before Lauder. Charles Coborn, for example, preceded him for a goodly number of years. It must be remembered that Lauder made his name at the beginning of this century. There was a wheen of comics and other music hall artists who were well known before he came, officially, upon the scene.

Few of the Scotch comics appeared in London. Those who had gone to the Great Metrollops were badly received, while Irish comedians were welcomed with open arms. A typical example of the Scotch comic at that time was Glasgow's Harry Linn, of whom it was said that Queen Victoria had dropped one of her favourite phrases, 'We are not amused', and admitted that he actually amused her. I have never been able to verify this story, but, if it is a legend, it is a long lasting one.

Harry Linn seems to have been a tall, thin man with a somewhat lugubrious face, perhaps a bit like our own great Tommy Lorne. He dressed in a travesty of the Victorian Scotch ensemble with a funny wee kilt and a large sporran, together with a scarlet uniform jacket and a Glengarry bonnet. His famous number was 'The Fattest Man in the Forty-Twa'. The Forty-Twa was the 42nd Highland Regiment.

The chorus of this masterpiece ran:

The win' may blaw, the cock may craw,
The rain may rain and the snaw may snaw,

> Ye couldnae frichten John McGraw,
>> The fattest man in the Forty-Twa.

By this time Harry Linn had been reduced to appearing at the 'Bursts', an immensely popular style of entertainment which was held in halls in various parts of Glasgow, including the large and sumptuous City Hall in the Candleriggs. The biggest 'Bursts' were made up of a 'Soirée, Concert and Ball'. It cost ninepence to attend the soirée and concert, and for another ninepence you could attend the ball as well.

The audience sat at long wooden tables and tea was served from huge urns. Each visitor received a large paper poke which contained buns, scones and cookies. When the audience were replete, the show started. The audience, by the way, carefully preserved their paper bags, because they were to become part of the entertainment.

If it was one of the big 'Bursts' the well-known accompanist, Charles R. Baptie, would take his seat at the piano, invariably greeted by a round of applause. The audience knew that, if anything went wrong, it would not be Mr Baptie's fault. The atmosphere in the hall was, in fact, critical. One well-known Scotch comic of the time was reported as saying, 'If they listen to you there, you can sing anywhere.' The young apprentice, Harry Lauder, appeared at one show with a rope hanging loosely round his neck. The chorus of his song went:

> I widnae laugh nor I widnae cry,
> Nor pay three wing for a tuppeny pie;
> But I'll hang masel' on this spot here
> A' for the sake o' Mary.

He got no further than the chorus when a voice came from the audience, 'For heaven's sake see and pu' the rope ticht!'

But when one of the top Glasgow comics appeared, he usually got a decent hearing. There was W.F. Frame, the Man U Know, who was now reaching his declining years but was still a favourite, especially with his song, 'A Lassie needs a Pairtner when the Nichts Grow Cauld'. Those in the audience who wanted to show their appreciation would blow up their paper pokes and burst them and, when explosions were heard all over the hall, you knew you had succeeded. There were, however, those in front who had kept bits of their food ration and expressed their disapproval by dunking the remains in their tea and throwing these soggy objects at the performer.

As time went on, W.F. Frame was one of the comedians who

W.F. Frame as 'Trooper Frame'. (SCOTTISH THEATRE ARCHIVES)

resented Lauder's rise to fame. Frame was still doing well in the minor music halls of Scotland and could get a good audience in certain Glasgow theatres. Lauder brought out his first book, *Harry Lauder at Home and on Tour,* in 1907 and ended his introduction by saying, 'If ye're no' pleased wi' this first attempt o' mine I'll never write anither book, mind I'm tellin' ye. And even if ye are pleased I'll never write anither.'

He wrote these words before he realised he was to be a best-seller. By April 1914, his book had sold 45,000 copies. This seemed to make W.F. Frame all the more jealous and he brought out *W.F. Frame's Songs and Stories.* I have a copy of his 'Latest Edition', published in 1912: criticism of Lauder is implicit in it although never mentioned openly. Frame describes himself on the cover as 'Phunniest of Phunny Phellows'.

One item in the penny pamphlet runs: 'One of Mr W.F. Frame's most cherished possessions is a letter from his old friend, Dan Leno, in which the late-lamented comedian wrote: "We are moving, so you can guess how we are situated. I looked for my pen and ink; found them rolled up in a night-shirt, packed away in the safe. Do send that white heather; we shall think so much of it coming to our new home (at Clapham park) I believe it means good luck. — Yours always, Dan."'

It was the done thing for Scotch comics to claim they knew Dan Leno, and there was even one of them, J.H. Anthony, father of the late Jack Anthony, who was billed as the 'Scottish Dan Leno'. His real name was Herbertson, so it's not surprising that he changed it for theatrical purposes. One of his repeated claims to fame in later years was that he had beaten Harry Lauder at a 'Bursts' competition and had a gold medal to show for it.

W.F. Frame reprints an obvious puff from the Hippodrome magazine for January 1903. It is entitled 'A Nicht wi' Frame at the Alhambra Theatre, London' and I give you the opening paragraph.

'"He is an innovation," said one of the Alhambra directors to us as we watched W.F. Frame from the auditorium of this great establishment on his opening night. What a success he made — echoes might have been heard far away on the Highland hills. It is no braggadocio to say it was a real "nicht wi' Frame". The lairds and the elders would have held their sides — the crofters would have said, "Frame's a wee bonnie laddie". He has come from the Brighton Hippodrome to the London Alhambra, and the sprig o' heather crowns his cap. Frame is as famous as the Macgregors — his name is a household word from John o' Groats to the farthest corner of the Scottish dominions. His quaint conceits, his inspiriting work refreshes us like a breezy blow on the top of Ben Nevis. Assuredly the most comical fellow we have seen in London since Frame came here before.'

Perhaps I should point out that, by the time these words appeared, Harry Lauder had been a success in London for two years. And perhaps that is the reason for the claim on one of Frame's pages — 'FRAME is the Originator of "HOOCH AYE" Songs.'

I'm sorry I never saw W.F. Frame but I recall he was still appearing in Glasgow music halls in the early 'twenties, by which time I calculate he must have been in his late sixties or early seventies. I was an apprentice chartered accountant at the time and I used to walk home every night from the office in St Vincent Street to my home at 7 Kennyhill Square. On the way I stopped at every theatrical poster I saw. There were a great many of them in those days and I recollect the W.F. Frame ones very clearly. They were notable for the number of times that the name Frame appeared.

A good Glasgow Scotch comic was Jack Lorimer, who was one of the very few who made a successful trip to the United States: he seems to have been the first Scottish music hall artist to make a success there. Jack Lorimer is little remembered today but he had a son named Maxwell Lorimer, who was destined for music hall fame. He is known today as one of the most individual comedians on the stage and also as an acclaimed actor. He does not appear in his father's image. He changed the name Maxwell to Max Wall and dropped the Lorimer altogether.

Other outstanding music hall performers of the time were J.B. Preston, a solid Scotch comic who didn't have to appear at the 'Bursts', J.M. Hamilton, a fine Scottish tenor who looked magnificent in the full Highland outfit but ended his days taking any kind of concert engagement he could get, and Hugh Ogilvie, the author of 'Hail Caledonia', which many people thought was a better Scottish national anthem than 'Scots Wha Hae'.

Hugh Ogilvie wrote 'Hail Caledonia' on a roll of wallpaper. He was a painter and decorator at the time and this was the only material he had to write on. It became such a success that he was able to give up the painting and decorating and go on the music hall stage as a singer. He was popular in Glasgow, although even then there were perfervid Scottish Nationalists who objected to the last line of 'Hail Caledonia', which went: 'Long rule Britannia, God save the King.'

Ogilvie refused to change the line, but eventually he found that his music hall engagements were not what they once were, particularly in Glasgow. So he simply decided to be a Scotch comic instead. He told a friend, 'I'll make far more money painting my nose red than I do as a singer.'

He did fairly well as a comedian but even better as an entrepreneur. He was able to tour shows all over Scotland, not only music hall programmes but the Fife Miner Players who performed the works of a fine dramatist who has just been rediscovered — Joe Corrie.

This case of a singer turning comic is not unusual. One example

19

is the case of Martin and Holbein. They were actually brothers and their name was Halfpenny. They were perhaps not in the front line but they were never out of a job and played the principal theatres as well as the minor halls. Pete Martin was the feed to Charlie Holbein who was one of the 'sad' comics, partly because he was not a well man. Pete also sang and had a fine tenor voice.

At the height of their success (an appearance in the Glasgow Empire) Charlie Holbein collapsed and never recovered. Pete Martin made the same decision as Hugh Ogilvie — to change from feed to comic. He made a good job of it, too, though you could tell that the audience were always waiting for him to sing!

THREE

THE LAUDER ENIGMA

IN THE 'TWENTIES OF this century a Scottish missionary and his wife were doing their best to take Christianity to China. Their name was Wynd, and their son, Oswald Wynd, is, under several different names, one of Scotland's best-known authors today. Their problems were those which beset any missionaries in a foreign field. They were trained to meet these problems and were not unduly worried by them.

But one day a terrible predicament arose. It was announced that a man named Harry Lauder was going to appear at the Imperial Theatre in Shanghai, where the Wynds were living. They knew that Lauder was the greatest stage entertainer the world had ever known. And the problem for Mr and Mrs Wynd was — should they go to see him at the Imperial Theatre?

The theatre, to missionaries, was the Temple of Beelzebub, but they dearly wanted to see this man from their own country and to hear his famous Scottish songs — 'I Love a Lassie', 'Roamin' in the Gloamin" and all the rest of them. Mrs Wynd was particularly worried because earthquakes were not uncommon in China and she quailed at the thought of an earthquake breaking up the Imperial Theatre in Shanghai, so that she might have to meet her Maker straight from a hotbed of sin. She and her husband talked and talked, until at last they decided that the call of Scotland, as represented by Harry Lauder, was irresistible. They booked two seats for the show.

If there were any other Westerners there, the Wynds didn't see them. They seemed to be surrounded by Chinese, and excited

Harry Lauder with Charlie Chaplin in Hollywood, *c.* 1915.
At this time, when America had yet to come into the war,
Lauder was raising funds in USA for British wounded soldiers.
He was knighted in 1919 for his tireless services
in entertaining and raising money for the troops.
(AUTHOR'S COLLECTION)

Chinese at that. When Lauder eventually appeared on the stage there was a great shout of welcome from the audience. Every song he sang was greeted with salvoes of applause, although the Wynds realised that the Chinese couldn't possibly understand, 'If it's a braw, bricht moonlicht nicht the nicht, ye're a' richt, ye ken!'

The Wynds went back to their mission happy and satisfied and never regretted that they had taken this daring, defiant step. Indeed, they felt better for having seen Harry Lauder.

Now let me take you into the days of the Second World War, when Sir Harry Lauder had long since retired, but was still a personality in the West of Scotland. He had built a new house, Lauder Ha', in the village of Strathaven, some sixteen miles south of Glasgow, and visitors from all over the world went to see him there.

At that time there was a funny wee theatre at Glasgow Cross called the Queen's. It had been a theatre since Victorian days and its presentations varied between the transpontine drama and fourth-rate music hall shows. During the late 'thirties and early 'forties it had built up a great reputation for its annual pantomime, a decidedly 'permissive' entertainment. The Glasgow Police did not approve and, when they found that no script of the pantomime had ever been sent to the Lord Chamberlain, they moved in.

The scripts were written by Frank Droy, one half of the duo, Frank and Doris Droy, who were the stars of the show. He duly sent a script to the Lord Chamberlain, who may have been surprised to receive a pantomime written in pencil in a school exercise book. The dialogue was all broad Glasgow of the type familiar today through the 'Parliamo Glasgow' appearances of yet another Scottish missionary, Stanley Baxter. To the consternation of the police, the Lord Chamberlain passed the script. This may have been because nobody in his department could understand it, or possibly because Frank Droy never thought it necessary to include descriptions of stage action in his oeuvre.

At the beginning of the war the best seats in the Queen's cost 1s 6d. The brave and the fair of Glasgow's society took up the Queen's with great gusto. Parties of young men in dinner jackets would be seen occupying a couple of rows of stalls before they went off to supper. Invariably there were at least two uniformed attendants watching the gilded youths closely in case they behaved in a manner not fitting for Glasgow Cross.

One evening Harry Ashton, the manager of the King's Theatre, went to see the Queen's Theatre pantomime. Mr Ashton was distinguished-looking, wore a monocle and dressed in style.

An attendant ushered him to his seat and Harry got the impression that the man was looking at him closely. It occurred to him that the attendant might know that he was the manager of the King's and have the impression he was 'slumming'. Harry bought a programme and studied it.

As he looked at the programme, he screwed his monocle into his weak eye. Soon he was conscious of the fact that the attendant had come down the aisle and was having another look at him. Mr Ashton decided that the attendant had maybe never seen a monocle in the Queen's Theatre before and wanted a closer view of it.

The attendant vanished but, just as the orchestra was tuning up, he reappeared at Harry Ashton's side. He leaned over conspiratorially and whispered, 'Ah jist thought ye'd like to know that Harry Lauder sat in that seat last night!'

That simple tribute to Lauder impresses me as much as the Scottish missionaries debating whether it was God's will that they should go to see a Scotch comic in the Imperial Theatre in Shanghai. And I know that even today, 35 years after he died, people in all walks of life will still produce programmes, posters, postcards and pictures to show that they saw Harry Lauder.

That is one side of the coin, an appropriate metaphor to use in the case of Lauder. It is difficult to separate the myth from the man. It can be said that there are two facts we are sure of. Harry Lauder was born in Portobello, near Edinburgh, on 4 August 1870. He died on 26 February 1950, in his eightieth year.

The Lauder myth is that he spread all over the world the idea of the Scot as mean, mostly drunk, wearing ridiculous clothes, a figure of derisive fun. I quote Professor David Daiches, a Scot himself, who wrote in his book *Scotch Whisky* that people 'in the second half of the nineteenth century (had) oddly mixed notions of the Scots as a nation of hairy-kneed, kilt-wearing consumers of whisky and haggis who sang songs about a wee hoose amang the heather. Harry Lauder was the apotheosis of this conception of Scotland'.

Professor Daiches is only one of many Scots who take this view. I don't know of any Scot who has been denigrated so expertly as Harry Lauder, although there was a time when Robert Burns was in the same class. Of course, the Scots have always been the greatest denigrators of the Scots. And what the denigrators can't stand is the idea that Lauder not only gave the world a false impression of the Scots, but did it for money!

If Lauder was giving the world a false idea of the Scot, he was doing it between 1900, when he made his first success, and 1907. By that time he was so established that he no longer had to wear comic costumes. Indeed, he had taken to character studies while there were still stage Irishmen, stage Jews, stage Americans and stage Frenchmen on the boards. All of them made fun of their own race, and for the life of me I can't see anything wrong with that.

There are those, however, who come to praise Lauder. Viscount Stuart of Findhorn wrote in his book, *Within the Fringe*, 'Harry Lauder, an Ayrshire (sic) miner with, as my father said, a "faultless true voice", was usually at the Tivoli in the Strand. Not only did he always fill the house, but he always brought it down single-handed.'

Chaliapin, the great Russian singer, said, 'When I want to listen to a perfect voice, I put on a record of Harry Lauder.'

Sir Hugh Robertson, the conductor of the world famous Glasgow Orpheus Choir, wrote in the choir magazine, the Lute, of Lauder's death in 1950:

'Harry Lauder! The little wee man with the twinkling eyes and the twinkling feet; the little wee man whose unerring sense of rhythm had carried him so bravely over so many years of brilliant music-making; the little wee man who, by native intelligence, had arrived at a concept of singing (as singing) far beyond the ken of most singers; the little wee man who, in singing, never forced, never exhibitionised, never got into a vocal fankle, never over-sang, never under-sang.

'The little wee man who, tutored simply by his innate sense of artistic proportion, worked at his words until each word became a living and shining thing, matched and mated, free and resilient, linked together into a veritable string of pearls.

'Yes, Harry could do this sort of thing as no other could or can — the glow of the heart and the light of the mind in every word and in every phrase. Questioned on one occasion, he replied — "That's what I'm paid for; the folk maun ken what I'm singin' aboot." And the folk kent, yes, even the English folk kent when they could not pretend wholly to understand.'

And, as I have already suggested, the Chinese folk kent too!

There was, of course, a dichotomy in Lauder's make-up. He sought privacy but he courted publicity. In his later years he couldn't bear to be ignored. When he was in his seventies he paid a visit to Edinburgh with his nephew, William Fraser. This was purely for pleasure but he wanted Edinburgh to know that Harry Lauder was there. When he went into the dining room of the

North British Hotel, Harry was irked because the head waiter didn't recognise him. Nor did any of the waiters greet him with the respectful, 'Good morning, Sir Harry' that he expected.

He sat through his lunch fuming because he was not the cynosure of neighbouring eyes. He got more and more irritable and William Fraser became quite alarmed. But nothing happened until the coffee was brought. Then Sir Harry took out a cigar and, although Fraser well knew he had a lighter in his waistcoat pocket, he went over to the nearest table, where two men were sitting, and asked them for a light. This did the trick. The business men were old enough to remember him and Harry came back to his table, almost satisfied.

Having tasted blood, Sir Harry let William Fraser pay the bill (he seldom carried money in later life) and led the way to the hotel entrance, which is pillared and wide and has several steps leading down into Princes Street. There, although his car was already at the edge of the pavement, Sir Harry stood and waited for recognition. He pointed one way down Princes Street and another way down the Leith Walk and it was all that Fraser could do to urge him into the car.

This may have been a throwback to earlier days when he was visiting big cities and towns with his niece, Greta Lauder, who was also his confidante, secretary and latterly comforter. Greta said that each time they arrived in a place of any size it was her duty to ring up all the hotels and ask Reception to page Sir Harry Lauder. So that at least the people in the hotels would know that Lauder was in town.

It was this publicity-seeking which was, of course, the reason for his spreading of the myth of his meanness. In these same hotels he would ask a page boy to get him a couple of daily papers, which then cost one penny each. He would give the page a threepenny-piece and, when the boy brought back the papers, Lauder would lift them from the salver and leave the odd penny on it. The page would naturally assume that this was his tip and he would be half way across the hotel lobby when a stentorian voice would roar, 'Page! Ye've forgotten ma change!'

The blushing boy would have to retrace his steps and hand over the penny, while all around people were nodding to each other and saying, 'Harry Lauder! Isn't that just like him?'

I met a man who was one of these page boys in the Lauder era. It had happened once or twice to him, so he was ready when Lauder asked him to bring a Glasgow Herald, which cost twopence, and gave him the customary threepenny-bit. The page boy put the penny change on his salver and covered it with the newspaper. Then he laid it down on a table beside Sir Harry.

Sure enough, there was the customary roar of 'Whaur's ma change, laddie?' and the page boy was able to return, lift the newspaper, and show the penny lying underneath.

One story that gained widespread publicity in London concerned the end of the successful revue, *Three Cheers*, in which Lauder starred with Ethel Levey. The show had played to packed houses for more than two years. On the last night, as he was walking out of the Shaftesbury Theatre, Lauder stopped at the stage-doorkeeper's box. 'Thank you very much for all you've done for me,' he said. 'There's a wee present for you.' And he handed the stage-doorkeeper an autographed picture postcard of himself.

What nobody knew at the time was that the stage-doorkeeper was in the act, and had been generously tipped by Harry Lauder in secret so the myth of Lauder's meanness could be perpetuated.

These 'typical Scot' stories were received with mixed feelings in Britain, but they were an enormous success in America. He was able to crack ancient Scottish jokes that were new to the Americans. For instance that when he wanted to fill his fountain-pen he always went to the bank where he kept his overdraft because it had better quality ink than you got in the post office.

When his autobiography, *Roamin' in the Gloamin'*, was serialised in the Saturday Evening Post in 1928, he wrote a special introduction for his American readers. (It's possible that he did not write these words, but merely inspired them. He had at least two ghost-writers, but would take over himself when he felt like it.)

He starts, '"When are you going to retire, Harry?" Why people all over the world should keep on asking this question of a young and strong man (he was 58 at the time) only anxious to do his job and save a shilling or two for his old age is beyond me! I don't know how the rumour about my retiral got abroad.

'If I ever come across the chap that started it I will give him a "bung on the broo"! It's not fair to a young comedian with a future before him and anxious to earn an honest but precarious living.

'Me retire! How do the people that ask me the question know that I have made enough money to retire on? Do they not stop to think that if I retired I would have to spend a lot of money without earning any? And that such a prospect, if all the tales about Harry Lauder be true, would be altogether too dreadful for him to contemplate!'

This rather sad stuff was apparently just what the Saturday Evening Post readers wanted. Elsewhere in the serialisation 'mean' stories about Lauder in America are injected.

When I read this, I think of the story of Edna Whistler, which I received from a friend of hers in New Jersey. Edna Whistler, a niece of the famous artist, was a young American soprano when she received an offer to join Harry Lauder on one of his all-round-America tours. Sometimes he took Scottish music hall artists and a pipe band with him, but most of his companies, over 22 years of touring, were almost entirely American. Edna Whistler was delighted with the offer and joined the 'Harry Lauder Special' train in New York. This train consisted of three coaches, a baggage car, a Pullman sleeping car for the company, and a parlour car for the Lauders and Harry's American agent, Will Morris.

Lauder was very proud of the fact that his parlour car was the 'Riva' saloon, which President Teddy Roosevelt used on his whistle-stop and other tours. Sarah Bernhardt and Adelina Patti had also used it in their day and Lauder never tired of explaining to visitors the importance of this parlour car.

The 'Harry Lauder Special' set out and the tour was going well. But one night, Edna Whistler became ill. When Sir Harry and Lady Lauder were told, they hurried from their bedrooms to the Pullman carriage. At once they realised that the soprano was very sick indeed and they insisted that she should be taken to occupy Lady Lauder's bed. Lady Lauder sat beside her and nursed her on the journey to the next city.

Meanwhile Sir Harry had succeeded in telegraphing to the next station and, when the train arrived, an ambulance was waiting to take her to hospital. Edna Whistler was in hospital for several weeks. As soon as she was well enough to understand, she was told that her place in the show was still open for her and that her train fare would be paid to whichever city the 'Harry Lauder Special' had reached by the time she was well. During all the time she was ill she was kept on the Lauder payroll, and Sir Harry paid all her hospital expenses. And then, when she did rejoin the company, she was asked not to say anything in public that would destroy Sir Harry's reputation!

On one occasion Lauder was appearing in the sadly lost Alhambra Theatre in Glasgow and the assistant manager, James Colquhoun, was paying an official visit to his dressing room. A minor Scotch comic, obviously down on his luck, called to see Lauder, who received him kindly and asked if things were any bet-

Sir Harry Lauder, on one of his regular trips to the USA,
being greeted on his arrival in New York by Sir Thomas Lipton,
the Scottish businessman and philanthropist.
(AUTHOR'S COLLECTION)

ter. When the wee comic said they weren't, Lauder went over to his waistcoat, hanging with his outdoor clothes on the dressing room wall, and pulled out five sovereigns. He pressed them on the comedian saying, 'Just you cheer up a bit. Things will come right for you yet.'

Secrecy was the word for Harry Lauder's benefactions. He kept a private list of people to whom he sent money regularly. He had an unerring nose at the same time for frauds, the panhandlers and the free-loaders. He had the charity concert 'racket' sized up. In the past many concerts were run for charity all right, but the artists were paid. He investigated each concert as it came along and, if other people were being paid, he demanded a fee too. This maybe explains a Letter to the Editor which appeared in a Glasgow evening newspaper.

'My brother-in-law was in the St Mungo Quartet and the Select Choir, and appeared quite often at the same concerts as Lauder. Many of the concerts were for charity, but Lauder had to get a fee. He wanted to hold the stage all the time. He didn't want anyone else to get a chance. In other words, he was a mean, pompous wee man.'

Well, when the 'mean, pompous wee man' was a miner in the Eddlewood Colliery at Hamilton he fell in love with his pit pony, Captain. He never forgot Captain throughout his life. When he became famous and rich he heard of measures being promoted for greater safety in the mines. So he made an additional appeal for legislation to reform the conditions under which pit ponies worked.

Lady Belhaven, of Wishaw House, near Hamilton, supported him. Together they put up such a case and enlisted so much support that the Home Secretary of the day put forward new legislation to look after the pit ponies as well as the miners. What the public never knew was that Harry Lauder was pumping his own money into the fund for making life easier for the ponies. He gave at least £1000 at a time when that was a tremendous sum of money — but on one condition: that nobody should know that the money came from Harry Lauder.

Throughout his long career Harry Lauder made many appearances in two of the top music halls in Glasgow, the Alhambra and the Empire. He was having a Monday morning rehearsal at the Empire and, being a knight by this time, deemed that it was not necessary to do more than sit in an armchair on the stage and go over his songs with the orchestra. He had a walking stick with him and, as the orchestra struck up, he started thumping his stick on the stage to give his timing.

This was too much for the conductor, Dr Henry Farmer, a highly accomplished musician and a noted Egyptologist to boot. He stopped his band and said, 'Excuse me, Sir Harry, but do you intend to do that stick thumping in your act.' Somewhat surprised, Sir Harry said he did not.

'Well,' said Dr Farmer, 'kindly don't do it now.'

He raised his baton and the rehearsal went on with no more thumping. But perhaps Lauder could be excused. The thumping came from his first appearances in London where he found that the orchestras seldom got his rhythm right. So he would bounce on to the stage with a wiggly stick and thump it to give the orchestra the correct timing. He'd kept up this practice for years but, as far as I know, no conductor had ever objected before Dr Farmer, whose doctorate, I should explain, was one of music.

I saw Harry Lauder's last professional appearance in Glasgow. Once again, it was at the Alhambra — a twice-nightly engagement for a week. It was booked out as soon as it was announced. I was a young reporter at the time, 1929, and was (if I haven't made it obvious already) theatre daft. I was delighted to be given the job of 'covering' the Alhambra that night. The programme consisted of a small troupe of dancing girls, some acrobats and a comedy conjurer in the first half; then, after the interval, the dancing girls appeared again and, when they had swirled around a bit, the Great Man came on himself for the rest of the show.

Looking round the audience, I could see that the majority were middle-aged to elderly people. Sir Harry then proceeded, once he had acknowledged the rapturous applause, to give exactly the same sort of performance he had given since Edwardian times, when things in the music hall moved at a comparatively easy pace.

He sang his first song, did the appropriate patter and finished with a rousing chorus, in which most of the audience joined. Then he made his exit and the band kept playing the song he had just sung until the green light flashed on in the orchestra pit, when the conductor took his band effortlessly into the next Lauder song on the programme. Sir Harry toddled on to the stage in the costume he had evidently been donning in the interval. This decidedly old-fashioned way of presenting his act was carried through twice more, until we had seen four of his 'characterisations'. Then he took several curtains from a largely appreciative audience, and finished off with one of his wee speeches.

There were not many young people in the audience but most of them, including me, were somewhat baffled. We were accustomed to Scotch comics, such as Tommy Lorne, who moved at a fairly rapid pace. My father had built up a large collection of Lauder records and I had always enjoyed them. Looking back on that farewell appearance, I feel I should have not been so critical, though I was by no means as critical as Stephen Watts in the Bulletin, who divided his review of the show into two columns — one detailing what he expected to see, and the other what he did see. I don't suppose that Harry Lauder bothered about what he would undoubtedly consider our juvenile outpourings.

After his farewell appearance in the Alhambra he gave many shows not only in Glasgow but in various parts of Scotland. These were all for charity and the fact that Lauder was advertised to appear always meant a packed audience. He also had a habit of turning up at the first night of each Glasgow pantomime, and that could number at least six or seven appearances. After suitable recognition from the stage and the audience, he would go behind the scenes and talk to the cast, invariably adjuring the comics to 'keep it clean'.

He was in his element when the Second World War broke out. He gave concerts to the troops and took on one war charity engagement after another. I recall a series of 'Garrison Theatre' shows which were put on every Sunday night in the King's Theatre. There was great cheering when Harry Lauder appeared. But he held up his hand for silence and said solemnly, 'Ladies and gentlemen, this is a great cause. But we must remember that this is the Sabbath.' And he sang, unaccompanied, 'Rocked in the cradle of the deep'.

That took the edge off the evening and the turns which followed had a hard row to hoe. It was the most remarkable example of the old stage saying, 'Follow that!', I have ever seen.

Sir Harry's final farewell appearance was in 1947. I owe the description of the scene to the assistant governor of a prison in England. In 1947 he was a member of a Scout Group Rover Crew in the Gorbals.

'We rejoiced,' he wrote, 'in the nickname, "the Diehards". To celebrate our twenty-fifth year of existence it was decided to put on a show at St Mungo Halls on the South Side of Glasgow in April, 1947.

'As Sir Harry had portrayed Dickson McCunn, leader of the Gorbals Diehards in a film of John Buchan's "Huntingtower", we

One of the last photographs to be taken of Sir Harry.
(STEPHENS ORR/SCOTTISH THEATRE ARCHIVES)

rather boldly decided that it would be appropriate and attractive (audience wise) if we could have Sir Harry along to open the show.

'Miss Greta Lauder was approached. At the time of the approach we were informed that Sir Harry had readily agreed, but his health was such that such agreement could only be tentative. In view of this we could not advertise his appearance, and as a result a most memorable performance was enjoyed by a relatively small audience.

'Sir Harry arrived on time, accompanied by his niece. Seeing him in the wings, I remember thinking how frail and almost helpless he looked.

'As soon as he reached the centre of the stage he became transformed. He stood there, looked at the audience and chuckled. He launched into a line or two of comic patter about being "a boy once masel'" and straight into a medley of the songs which he had made his own. In all he sang about eight of his, and the audience's favourites, before ending with "The End of the Road". There was no mike, yet his voice was heard clear and strong in all parts of the hall.

'The quality of the applause made up for lack of quantity in the audience.

'There was one note of pathos. When the cheering subsided, the grand old man stood there for a moment and then began to repeat his opening chuckle and patter.

'I was not in the wings at that moment, but I understand that Greta who, with others, had been greatly moved by the performance, sobbed, "Please someone, bring him off." The Group Scoutmaster dashed on stage and made a presentation of a small statuette of a Boy Scout, Sir Harry's fee for a great performance, which he would have repeated had he not been interrupted.

'I have always considered that this relatively unknown appearance of Sir Harry Lauder was typical of the man who created a myth of the canny Scot, but was in reality a most kind and generous person.'

Sir Harry Lauder was in his 77th year when he made what was his last appearance on any stage at this concert. He died less than three years later.

It would be wrong to leave the man who was called by Winston Churchill at a meeting in Edinburgh, 'your grand old Scottish minstrel', on a down-beat. Let me end this effort at an analysis of the man who was Harry Lauder with a true story of a meeting which had a most remarkable ending.

One evening, when he was appearing in an early engagement in the Alhambra, he was asked if he would see a song writer called Will Fyffe. He graciously acceded and young Mr Fyffe was ushered into his dressing room. The nervous young man explained that he and his wife were doing a comedy duo act and that he had written a song which he felt sure was just made for Sir Harry Lauder. And he handed over a manuscript which contained the words and music of a song entitled 'I Belong to Glasgow'.

Sir Harry read and reread the manuscript. Then he shook his head and said, 'No, it's all right in its way but it's no' for me. I never sing songs in praise of drink.'

This took Will Fyffe aback. 'But Sir Harry,' he said, 'what about your song "A Wee Deoch an' Doris". Isn't that praising drink?'

'Not the way *I* sing it,' said Lauder. 'Listen.' And he sang the first two lines of the song —

'Just a *wee* deoch an' doris, just a *wee* yin, that's a'.

Just a *wee* deoch an' doris, before ye gang awa'.'

Will Fyffe looked slightly baffled, and Lauder said, 'You see, I put all the stress on the word "wee" so, instead of being a song that's praising drink, it's really warning people against taking too much.'

Thus Sir Harry Lauder turned down a song which became as popular as any of his own. And thus he helped Will Fyffe to success without knowing it. I'm sure that, when 'I Belong to Glasgow' did succeed, Sir Harry still thought he was right. He nearly always did.

FOUR

FYFFE
AND
LORNE

THE FUNNIEST MAN I have ever seen in a Glasgow music hall was Grock, the Swiss musical clown, who flounced out of Britain because of our tax system and never came back. I should really say 'the funniest man I have ever seen in my life' and I have seen funny men in most parts of the world. But almost equal with him was a Glasgow chap called Hugh Corcoran. He is perhaps better known as Tommy Lorne, a name much quoted in local theatrical circles, though most of those who quote him are too young to have ever seen him.

My father didn't know Lloyd George, but he did know Tommy Lorne. He knew him as Hugh Corcoran, because young Hugh was in the draughtman's department in the Steel Company of Scotland's Blochairn Works, of which my father was secretary. One night he was working late in his office when he heard a peculiar rhythmic sound coming from the room above.

He decided to investigate and went upstairs. He was not surprised to see a light in the draughtsman's department because he knew two of the apprentices were working there. The rhythmic thumping grew louder and my father threw open the door to find Hugh Corcoran and the other apprentice practising tap dancing. That was how Tommy Lorne lost his first job.

He didn't worry overmuch because he was determined to go on the stage. His determination succeeded, for Harry McKelvie, the owner of the Royal Princess's Theatre in the Gorbals and the Palace Music Hall next door, saw him as a young comic and realised his potentialities. He was appearing with a partner and they kept changing the name of the act so that they could draw the dole at the same time.

McKelvie took Hugh Corcoran over and tried him out in the Palace and on tour and, when he saw that his apprentice comic was ready, he decided to put him into the prestigious Princess's pantomime. The first thing the boy would need was a new name. At the time Hugh Corcoran's ideal comedian was a top English performer whose stage name was Tom E. Hughes. Hughes did a tramp act and was very funny.

So, when the bill printer 'phoned the Palace and asked for the new Corcoran name, McKelvie said 'Tom E. Lorne'. The printer misunderstood and, when the bills arrived at the theatre, instead of Tom E. Lorne there appeared Tommy Lorne. McKelvie refused to have the bills reprinted and so Hugh Corcoran stayed Tommy Lorne for the rest of his all too brief life.

Harry McKelvie produced his own pantomimes. They were done on a scale which is impossible now, except in London. The chorus numbered a hundred but there were only twenty real chorus girls in the line up, professionals, most of them from London. They occupied the first two rows of the chorus and behind them were eighty local girls, some of whom could dance, but those at the back were enthusiastic amateurs who learned some basic steps and the words of the choruses. Nobody really saw them, except their relatives in the upper circle and gallery.

With the exception of the villain, who was always a London actor named John F. Traynor, and the principal boy, most of the cast were Scottish. When McKelvie decided to launch Tommy Lorne, he got a first-class feed who called himself Bret Harte. He had been in a double act with his wife, Dora Lindsay, but she had left him to do her very successful comedienne act on her own.

Bret Harte was a master of timing, which is very important in feeds. If he felt that Lorne was lagging he'd say *sotto voce*, 'Quicker, comic, quicker.' Tommy learned a lot from Bret Harte and his timing became immaculate. He also had the advantage of looking very funny. He was tall and thin and he had what can only be described as a remarkable face. He had only to come on to the stage to set the audience in a roar.

He had a strange, high-pitched voice and his Glasgow dialect was rich. Wanting to reprove someone on the stage, he would say, 'Ah'll get ye! An' if Ah don't get ye, the coos'll get ye!' (This is perhaps a good example of the old adage, 'It's not so much what he says as the way he says it.')

Tommy Lorne
(SCOTTISH THEATRE ARCHIVES)

In a couple of years Tommy Lorne had become a star in Glasgow and it was difficult to get seats in the Princess's, even though the pantomimes broke all British records for long runs. Jerry Desmonde once said of the Princess's, 'It's the only pantomime I know where you start it wearing a fur coat and end wearing a straw hat.'

At the end of each season Harry McKelvie would tour the dressing rooms on the last night. If he looked into your room and said, 'See you next year', you knew you were engaged. He didn't bother with contracts.

The Pavilion Music Hall looked with envious eyes on the Princess's. They ran a twice-nightly pantomime each winter and an emissary approached Lorne with an offer of a much bigger salary than he was getting at the Princess's. Lorne was tempted but he worried about McKelvie's farewell, 'See you next year, comic.' He explained this to the emissary, who assured him that lawyers would look into the case and make sure his move to the Pavilion would be absolutely legal. Lorne was inexperienced enough to accept this at face value and was quite unprepared for the wrath which descended when McKelvie heard about it.

No lawyers had looked into the case and the Pavilion people were seriously in the wrong. McKelvie could have demanded Lorne's return to the Princess's but he chose instead to arrange that the Pavilion management would pay the equivalent of Lorne's Princess's salary to McKelvie every week of the pantomime's run. This was agreed and every week Harry McKelvie paid the money into one of the charities he supported. Nor did he worry over much about Lorne's defection, for he was already nursing a new young comic by the name of Dave Bruce.

Despite all the stramash, Tommy Lorne was a great success at the Pavilion. So much so that the posh pantomime place in Glasgow, the Theatre Royal, which had always used English comedians such as George Robey, Harry Weldon, Jay Laurier and Billy Merson, made the momentous decision to present their first Scotch comic, Tommy Lorne. They had used Scotch comics before, but always in minor roles.

Lorne adapted to the different atmosphere with instant success. He had the sense to hire more sophisticated script writers and he worked well with the producers brought up from London. Meanwhile, at the Princess's, Harry McKelvie had found himself in unexpected difficulties. When his new comic, Dave Bruce, turned up for their first pantomime discussion, McKelvie said, 'Right! Where are your songs, comic?' Bruce handed over one or two published song sheets and McKelvie was aghast. His comics always provided their own original songs. Bruce was told to go away and return with songs written for him.

This was done, but Dave Bruce was what was known in the trade as a 'lazy' comic. If he bounced on to the stage and started his act and didn't get the laughs he expected he just didn't bother trying any more. He was a very easy going chap and McKelvie liked him. So, at the end of the season, he got the usual nod from Harry who, however, had other plans afoot.

There was no television in those days (in Scotland, at least) and radio was the craze. So McKelvie broke the habits of a lifetime and engaged a London comedian called Syd Walker, who had a very successful radio series, as principal comic, in the hope that this would inspire Bruce to greater things. He brought other comedians in. As Tommy Morgan said, 'That was the year that Harry McKelvie threw on the comics in bundles of six!' He and his partner, Tommy Yorke, got their first and only engagement at the Princess's in that pantomime.

It was not a flop, for Princess's patrons were a loyal crowd. But in McKelvie's eyes it was a sore disappointment. Fortunately, he had picked yet another young Scotch comic, George West, after trying him out in the sticks, put him into the next Princess's pantomime. He was to be the Princess's comic for the next sixteen years.

But all was not well with Tommy Lorne either. He continued to be the success of the Theatre Royal pantomime and there came a time when he signed a new contract for a salary of £250 a week (a very large sum at that time) plus a percentage of the box office takings. For several weeks he received £275 and yet the theatre was packed every night. He mentioned this to a friend, who worked out the percentage according to Tommy and came up with the conclusion that he should be receiving, on these terms, £400 a week.

Lorne took this up with the manager of the Theatre Royal, who pointed out that he had overlooked the small print in the contract, which said that he was entitled to his salary, plus percentage, but not to exceed £275 a week.

He played the rest of the pantomime with this grudge at the back of his mind and it was about then, according to Lorne watchers, that he started to drink. Up till then he had been a teetotaller and a non-smoker.

By this time Lorne had an excellent feed, W.S. Percy, an English musical comedy actor who was very small and a first-class foil. Apart from pantomime, Lorne took out his own touring revues and covered a large number of theatres in the North of England. He used to say, 'Me and Jack Buchanan are the only ones who can tour in England because we can both talk English.' It was then that his drinking became evident. The revues were twice nightly and every now and again W.S. Percy had to become the comedian for the second performance. Lorne's contract for the Theatre Royal pantomime was not renewed. He became the forgotten comic.

But Tommy Lorne still had the sense to know that drink was his problem and he must conquer it. When he succeeded, he decided to make a return to the stage. He raised enough money to put on a big-scale pantomine in Inverness. It was a success and he then took it on tour to the principal Scottish theatres, ending with two weeks at the Glasgow Empire. I am glad to say I was in the audience on his first night. The place was packed and the reception for Tommy Lorne was the biggest I have ever heard in that theatre. The King had come back. God save the King!

The result was that the Theatre Royal asked him to return to the fold and he signed a contract to appear in the next year's pantomime on the best terms he had ever had. That summer he contracted a serious illness and died. Huge crowds attended his funeral at Kirkintilloch. Tommy Lorne was a much loved man.

It's odd to think that an equally loved man, Will Fyffe, was a contemporary of Tommy Lorne. Fyffe, as far as being a music hall star was concerned, was what clever people call a late developer. But, of course, he lived much longer than Lorne, so it wasn't usually realised that they were of the same vintage.

I first saw Will Fyffe in the Pavilion Theatre. He had just made his big hit in London with 'I Belong to Glasgow' and he was billed as 'The Great New Scottish Character Comedian'. He slew the audience. He was a bit like Harry Lauder, but didn't have such a good voice. On the other hand, his character studies had more depths than Lauder's.

Fyffe seemed, though it seems odd to say it now, a modern comedian. His drunk man singing 'I Belong to Glasgow' was absolutely superb. James Agate put it perfectly when he wrote of Will Fyffe that he was not just impersonating a drunk — he was a drunk man trying to convince his hearers that he was sober.

Oddly enough, I can't recollect now what his other songs were that night, but whatever he did was good, with the perfect timing of the real actor. And, though his voice was maybe not up to the Lauder standard, it was a good voice for the type of songs he sang. His patter was much better than Lauder's, but that was because Lauder was still sticking to the same patter which he had used since the beginning of the century.

Fyffe was born in Dundee, son of Jack Fyffe, a good actor-manager who ran a penny geggie. Penny geggies came in all shapes and sizes and some of them were not much more than tents. Jack Fyffe's geggie was a portable wooden theatre, a comparatively substantial affair when judged by the standard of other geggies.

He was considered to be one of the best 'Rob Roys' in Scotland and, according to Will Fyffe, the company was a pretty good one. Incidentally, audiences paid more than a penny to get into Fyffe's geggie but, whatever you paid, the show was still called a penny geggie.

They toured mainly in the small towns of Central Scotland and sometimes ventured into the Highlands and the North-East. They would put on a tragedy, a comedy and a farce. If it was a holiday in the area and good audiences could be expected, they might put on anything from two to four performances in the afternoon and evening. They cut the plays like mad. *Rob Roy* could be done in half-an-hour by the simple method of leaving out the songs. Apart from such Scottish classics as *Rob Roy* and *Jeannie Deans*, they went in strongly for such thrillers as *The Face at the Window, The Silver King, Burke and Hare* and *Maria Marten, or the Murder in the Red Barn.*

Will Fyffe told me he started acting in his father's geggie about the age of twelve, though he'd appeared in children's parts before that. By the time he was fifteen he was a fully fledged member of the company, taking the parts of old men, young women and any character his father decided he should play. Charlie Kemble, the great music hall veteran, said he saw Will Fyffe appearing as Polonius in a forty-minute version of *Hamlet.* He was sixteen at the time.

His biggest memory, he told me, was when the geggie was appearing at Perth. They'd put up their theatre on the South Inch, close to the wide and fast flowing River Tay. Running a geggie was rather like running a small travelling circus. As soon as the company arrived at the selected site, the material would be unloaded and the whole cast, actresses included, would proceed to erect it, just as the circus put up their Big Top, however wee it may actually be.

At the final performance on a site the whole company would dismantle the geggie and pack it on the truck for its journey to the next place. Will Fyffe was a small and wiry boy and just the perfect person to sclim to the top of the geggie and attend to the unbolting and unscrewing of the roof from its walls.

On this last night at Perth there was a terrible storm and the actors had to shout their heads off to be heard above the wind, the lashing rain and the roaring of the swollen River Tay. But work had to be done and young Will Fyffe got a leg up to the geggie roof, holding on like grim death. There came an even bigger blast than any faced that night, the portable theatre disintegrated and most of it, including the boy on the roof, was swept into the river.

Will held on desperately. He couldn't swim and conditions were so bad that he could hardly see. He seemed to be completely out of contact with his father and the other geggie people. Actually they were running along the river bank chasing him and the roof.

There is a point where an island divides the Tay in two and by the mercy of God the remains of the geggie were swept by the river on to the island shore. Will had some bruises, was soaked to the skin and frightened as he had never been in his life. But he was safe and sat amid the wreckage shivering until he was rescued by his family and friends.

'The only trouble,' he said to me many years later when he told me this story in his Theatre Royal pantomime dressing room, 'was that, by the way they were all pulling the bits of the geggie out of the river, it was more important than I was!'

The geggies were doomed when the favourite travelling show in Scotland became the moving picture. Jack Fyffe had to give up because he was getting too old for the demanding travelling and for the leading parts. Will Fyffe decided to become a Scotch comic, because he'd always preferred the comedy parts in them.

It was a hard life, but he was encouraged by Ben Popplewell, the owner of the Gaiety Theatre at Ayr, and eventually made it to London and fame. Few members of the audience realised that he was partially deaf in one ear, and so did most of his numbers with his good ear towards them. He made the physical position look perfectly natural. But I must say that, when he appeared in big Glasgow pantomimes at the Theatre Royal, and even bigger ones at the Alhambra, he had scenes in which he had to face the audience and it didn't appear to incommode him in the least.

The Spice of Life, the book on variety written by the famous London theatrical agent, George Foster, the man who guided Harry Lauder when he rose to fame, called Will Fyffe 'the natural successor to Lauder', which was very high praise indeed.

As far as Glasgow was concerned, Will Fyffe had an equivalent success to Lauder's. His every appearance in city theatres was a sell-out. This caused some concern in two major pantomime theatres — the Royal and the Alhambra. The Alhambra management became acutely conscious that London big names were not attracting as big audiences as three other theatres were doing in the pantomime season. It must be remembered that Glasgow was then the centre of pantomime in the whole of Britain. I recall when we had nineteen theatres in Glasgow. But even when we were down to eleven, nine of them had pantomimes.

The most successful pantomime in Glasgow was, as I have already mentioned, the Royal Princess's Theatre in the Gorbals. Almost as successful was the Coliseum Theatre, also on the South Side. Then came the Pavilion in Renfield Street. Fourth was the Theatre Royal (now the beautiful home of Scottish Opera). When the Alhambra, proud of its former Julian Wylie pantomime successes, examined the situation, they could come to only one conclusion — their successful rivals had one outstanding thing in common. Their stars were Scotch comics. It was the same in the second rank of theatres — the Pavilion, the Metropole, the Empire, the Empress, the Queen's, all had Scotch comics.

It was around this time that Dame Sybil Thorndike and her husband, Sir Lewis Casson, were appearing in the Citizens' Theatre, then directed by their son, John Casson. After seeing a Metropole production, Sir Lewis announced publicly, 'The national theatre of Scotland is pantomime.' I don't know whether his wife agreed with him or not, but she had already made a successful appearance as principal boy in George Bernard Shaw's *Saint Joan* — in the title role, no less.

Realising the change in taste, the management of the Theatre Royal engaged Will Fyffe as their star. To say that he was a terrific success is understating it. He slew the audience every night. It was then that he introduced 'Daft Sandy', a moving and deeply felt study of a dafty, with all a dafty's hidden intelligence.

In my seventy years experience of theatre going, I've seldom seen such audience reaction as there was to Daft Sandy in the Theatre Royal. Will Fyffe got an ovation every night. Sure enough, the performance had its sentimental points too and there wasn't a dry eye in the house, but it was much more than sentimental. It was a wonderful, appealing study of a young man who had deep feelings but wasn't able to express them. If I had to pick Will Fyffe's greatest stage achievement, I would choose 'Daft Sandy'.

The Alhambra company, a very rich one, bided their time and then, at the right moment, they bought Will Fyffe. They teamed him up with a very successful Aberdeen comic, Harry Gordon. They had used Harry Gordon before, notably in a pantomime at the beginning of the Second World War, along with fellow comic Alec Finlay, and with Evelyn Laye as Prince Charming in *Cinderella*.

It was the winter of 1939-40 and people had no idea when the bombs were going to fall. In the event, Glasgow got off comparatively lightly compared to London, Coventry and Clydebank, but who could tell at that time? Evelyn Laye was engaged as principal boy for £2000 a week — an immense salary in those days. Not only that, but she had an arrangement with the management that, if the Alhambra was bombed, her salary would continue for the length of the arranged run.

As it turned out, the performances were occasionally interrupted by air raid alerts, but the audience stayed put (except for those who made a sudden exit to the bar) and nothing ever happened, except the cheer which was invariably raised when the 'All Clear' was sounded.

I must say that I have never seen a principal boy like Evelyn

Several faces of the incomparable Will Fyffe,
including St Mungo and 'Dr MacGregor and his wee black bag'.
(STEPHENS ORR/SCOTTISH THEATRE ARCHIVES)

Laye in that pantomime. She pursued Cinderella like a wolf and there were times when you felt that rape was imminent. I asked her about her characterisation and Miss Laye replied, 'Oh, I just follow what I've seen Frank doing.' Frank was Frank Lawton, her husband, and a good actor in his own right.

So the Alhambra had their new team of Will Fyffe and Harry Gordon. They were an immediate success. Fyffe played the male comic and Gordon was always the dame. They seemed to have some kind of empathy, though they were very different in real life. I can't remember a couple of comics better suited to each other.

Apart from pantomime, Will Fyffe was kept so busy with stage and film work that he complained he hadn't enough time for fishing. On the music hall side there was quite a sensation when he signed up to be the star of a new edition of *Earl Carroll's Vanities* on Broadway. There was an even bigger sensation when, after about a week, he cancelled his contract and came back to Scotland.

In those days many Scots commuted regularly between Glasgow and New York by Anchor Liner. You went down Kelvinhaugh Street, boarded the liner at Yorkhill Quay and, after several days of living like a millionaire, you left the liner just fornenst the Statue of Liberty. The voyage took under a week and I recall going to Yorkhill Quay to meet the Anchor liner which was bringing Will Fyffe back from New York after his dramatic exit from the Earl Carroll show.

In his cabin Fyffe was quite open about it. His contract meant that, as the star, all he had to do was make two appearances in the whole evening — each time doing one of his well-known numbers with patter. He was not connected with the main framework of the show.

He rehearsed his act on the Broadway stage without seeing anything else. It was only on the first night, standing in the wings, that he realised (in his own words) it was 'a dirty show'. Doubtless we'd think nothing of it now, since we've seen pretty well all of the dirt. But Fyffe took it very seriously indeed. He watched it for a night or two and decided it was not for him.

His walk out of the show caused a sensation in New York. The newspapers were full of it, and Walter Winchell was particularly scathing. When someone in the Fyffe entourage saw the Winchell story, he noticed there was a peculiar 'artistic' border round it. He examined it through a magnifying glass and found that it was a script reading 'Will Fyffe is a kike' all the way round the piece. Kike, of course, meant Jew. Will Fyffe laughed when he told me this in his cabin and said, 'I sent a postcard to Walter Winchell saying, "Walter Winchell is a liar", and I didn't put a stamp on it!'

This episode didn't do Will Fyffe any harm in the USA. He continued to do stage work and made a great many films, including a comedy series with an American star named Will Mahoney. Mahoney, like other American stars, made the ritual appearance at the Empire Theatre in Glasgow. I can't recollect the details of his act but I know that it finished with him playing the pop music of the time by dancing on a giant xylophone which occupied the whole stage.

My last personal meeting with Will Fyffe was at the Cot House Hotel at Kilmun on the Firth of Clyde. It stands at the top of the Holy Loch, now occupied by the American Polaris nuclear submarine base. The Cot Inn was a favourite howff of mine and I was there one wintry afternoon when a large limousine drove up and out stepped Will Fyffe.

He was starring with Harry Gordon in the Alhambra pantomime and, from what he said to me, I gathered that he'd felt like getting away from Glasgow and had ordered the car to take him down to the Cowal coast. We drank together in the Cot House bar and I congratulated him on the success of his pantomime. He was remarkably apathetic about it, though I'd seen him being his customary charismatic self on the stage. He said how well he got on with Harry Gordon but seemed to indicate that his heart was not in the show. It surprised me because I've always found that theatrical people respond immediately to praise, let alone flattery. The feeling I had then about Will Fyffe was one of deep despondence.

That was his last pantomime. He was already engaged to return to the Alhambra for the following season in *Humpty Dumpty*. The opening scene of this pantomime was to show Humpty Dumpty sitting on a high wall. Behind it the audience would see the flags and the bayonets and the top trappings of all the King's horses and all the King's men. Then would come a crash coinciding with a black-out.

When the curtains opened again it was in full light and Humpty Dumpty was to enter in disarray, with bits of the egg still sticking round him. He would look dolefully at the audience and say, 'Ah fell!'

During the autumn the script of *Humpty Dumpty* was sent to Will Fyffe at the hotel which he had bought at St Andrews (next to fishing, his favourite pursuit was golf). Rusack's Hotel was right on the Old Course and one of the best of the caravanserai in that part of the world. There was a fashion then for comedians who had made a lot of money to invest in a hotel or inn. This was not always a successful investment and it's notable that Harry Lauder never bought a hotel.

Will Fyffe's own suite looked directly on to the golf course and, if he wasn't playing, he was often watching the games spread out before him from a balcony some two storeys above ground level. No one knows what happened on this particular day but his body was found below the balcony. He had been killed outright. There were the inevitable rumours of suicide but it was pointed out that he had been suffering from ear trouble for years and it was possible that he had fallen from the balcony under the influence of this illness.

After the sensation, the Alhambra had to look at things from the point of view of their pantomime production. There was nobody quite like Will Fyffe (I mean in appearance and attitude), but there was one first-class comedian who, they felt, would work well with Harry Gordon. He was young Alec Finlay.

And so Alec Finlay was engaged for *Humpty Dumpty*, to play Will Fyffe's role. Alec knew of the circumstances of Fyffe's death and, since he was a Fyffe aficianado, took the situation very personally. So, on the first night, he stood in the Alhambra wings, ready to make his entrance as the somewhat eggshelled Humpty Dumpty.

He waddled on to the stage and said his opening line, 'Ah fell!' And, remembering what had happened to Will Fyffe, burst into tears. The audience, thinking this was acting, gave him a great round of applause. It was some time before the clapping died down and it was enough for Alec Finlay to recover himself and go on with the show.

During the long run of the pantomime Alec adjusted himself to the role, helped considerably by Harry Gordon, who was a most co-operative comic. At the end of *Humpty Dumpty* he was put under contract to the Alhambra and spent the next sixteen years of pantomime there.

Alec Finlay took over the Will Fyffe role, but he had been known for some time as the 'Pocket Lauder'. He was, by the way, one of the few Scotch comics who used his real name. He was christened Alexander Laing Finlay and was a native of Glasgow. His first stamping ground was the Band of Hope, Govanhill branch. When there was a concert, the boys and girls handed in their names for songs, recitations or dances. Alec thought he was very clever when he handed in the name of his pal, so as to embarrass him. The pal went on to the platform and stammered out a poem. But the next name to be called out was Alec's. His pal had double-crossed him. When young Alec got on to the Band of Hope platform, he didn't know what to do. Then he remembered a gramophone record of Harry Lauder's that they had in his home. He walked around the stage, singing this song and doing the patter in parrot-like fashion. He had never seen Lauder in his life.

The superintendent of the Band of Hope was so struck by this performance that he got Alec a kilt and a crooked stick. Alec toured Bands of Hope all over Glasgow and it was then he got the name of the Pocket Lauder. Years later he saw Sir Harry Lauder for the first time and was amazed how close he had got to the original. It just shows how much there is of Lauder in his records.

When he left school he became an office boy with a firm of flour merchants, and later was an apprentice engineer. But young Alec wore out his mother's linoleum learning how to dance. He teamed up with a chap called Ronnie Boyd. They made their first appearance at a matinee for unemployed at the Queen's Theatre, and got the bird. After rehearsing for six months, Finlay and Ronald were booked for three nights.

Success, in a manner of speaking, came for Alec when he joined the Frolics Concert Party, landed in Millport, and went to Ayr, where Charlie Kemble taught him a few things and he met Rita André, a young Glasgow dancer who duly became Mrs Finlay. Alec and Rita got engaged and started a double act. They joined up with Billy Lester and Dan Campbell to run a pantomime which toured Scotland for sixteen weeks and surprised everybody, including the promoters. But their own country didn't seem to hold a great deal for Finlay and André, so they decided to try London.

The London agents were polite but firm. There was no work. One day Finlay and André decided to go back to Glasgow by the 9 p.m. train. Just for a baur, Alec went along to an agent at 5 p.m. He was told they could have an audition from Sir Oswald Stoll at Shepherd's Bush. Alec and Rita cancelled their train reservations, stayed, and were one of two turns picked by Sir Oswald out of 26.

After this the duo did quite well. While they were appearing at Shepherd's Bush, they were staying at Clapham with Mrs Allan, mother of Ella Logan, the Glasgow-born Hollywood star. They took occasional outside engagements as well, and one night they were fixed to appear at the Variety Golfing Society Dinner in the

Finlay and André (H. KEMP HOLDINGS/SCOTTISH FILM ARCHIVE) and
Alec Finlay in an acting role, as the Scots undertaker.
(STEPHENS ORR/SCOTTISH THEATRE ARCHIVES)

Park Lane Hotel. Somehow or other, between Shepherd's Bush, Clapham and the Park Lane, Alec Finlay, who prided himself on his immaculate appearance, mislaid his evening dress trousers. He found himself at the Park Lane Hotel with everything but the pants. He didn't know what to do, but his wife suggested that he should put on his Lauder kilt in place of the trousers. 'You're supposed to be a comic,' she said. 'Prove it.'

Rather against his will, Alec went on the stage in his top hat, his white tie, his tail coat and his kilt and the Variety Golfing Society loved it. Rita gave him the name of 'Scotland's gentleman', and Harold Walden, comedian and football internationalist, wrote a song for him. It was 'In my top hat, my white tie, my tail coat, and my kilt.'

Thus inspired, Alec set himself to learn to play the bagpipes. The first time he played the pipes on the stage, he sent two sea lions (the following turn) into hysterics. He was an instant success. For two years he practised dancing and playing the pipes at the same time. He claimed to be the only man in the world who could do this ('I'm the only one daft enough to try') until somebody wrote a letter to the Radio Times to say that her husband could do it, too.

Finlay joined Ben Lyons and Bebe Daniels for a tour of South Africa, appeared all over the place in England, and then came back to his home town of Glasgow, where he was hailed as a 'discovery'. He went over to Belfast (a happy hunting ground for Scotch comics) and received a silver cup for breaking all records at the Opera House by staying there for $8\frac{1}{2}$ months.

He'd just arranged to tour Australia and New Zealand when the Second World War started. Then he was involved in plans to star in pantomime with Jessie Matthews in London, but Miss Matthews went to America, which was a much safer place. During the early war years I saw him in pantomime in Dundee, and hundreds of weans were crying because they couldn't get in to the matinee.

I like Charlie Kemble's remark when he saw Harry Lauder appearing in a big charity show given by the principal Scotch comics in the Empire Theatre. 'D'ye know,' said Charlie, 'he gets more like Alec Finlay every day!'

Alec Finlay was, perhaps, not one of the great Scotch comics, but he had his own niche and he filled it well. Certainly the Alhambra management were never sorry that they had engaged the Pocket Lauder to take over from Will Fyffe.

NORTHERN LIGHTS

Harry Gordon was unquestionably one of Scotland's finest pantomime dames, but there were times when I felt he was, perhaps, uncomfortably near the real thing. In each pantomime he appeared at least once in an immaculate woman's outfit. Indeed, he almost set the fashion for the blue-rinsed ladies of the West of Scotland. I hasten to add that this is not a snide comment on his masculinity, for he was eminently heterosexual. It was just an indiosyncracy of his.

Another contemporary dame caricatured women unmercifully. His name was G.S. Melvin and, like Will Fyffe, he came from Dundee. He was the Scotsman who became an illustrious English comedian, just as Charlie Coborn did. He started off as a Highland dancer and won medals at all the Highland Games. This was to become useful to him when he went on to the stage.

He came to Glasgow to star as the dame in the Theatre Royal pantomime. He was, as I've indicated, the grotesque type of dame but he was remarkable for the mobility of his body and the lightness of his feet, a legacy, obviously, from his Highland dancing days. The highlight of his performance at the Royal was his appearance as the Girl Guide to end all Girl Guides.

At that time what we would call today 'commercials' were common in pantomime, notably from the principal comics. I have seen Tommy Lorne stagger across the stage, carrying a giant bottle of HP Sauce for no apparent reason. But G.S. Melvin, when he was in Glasgow, told me one of the most remarkable tales of advertising and art.

Harry Gordon (STEPHENS ORR/SCOTTISH THEATRE ARCHIVES)

When he first started doing well, Melvin had an act in which he told a story about whisky. When he did this, he always mentioned Black and White. One night, when he was in his dressing room, G.S. Melvin received a card from a man who represented a whisky which I shall call Tartan Label.

The comedian asked the whisky representative in. 'You don't need to tell me unless you like,' said the whisky man, 'but how much are Black and White paying you to mention their name in that whisky story of yours?'

Melvin was amazed. 'They're not paying me anything,' he said. 'I just happen to mention Black and White when I tell the story, that's all.'

The whisky man rubbed his hands with glee. 'Well, Mr Melvin,' he said, 'perhaps we can do business. We're pushing Tartan Label in every possible way just now. If you're prepared to say Tartan Label instead of Black and White every time you tell that story, my firm will be delighted to send you a cheque every week and a case of a dozen bottles of Tartan Label once a month.'

Well, what would you do, chum? It meant nothing to Melvin to change the name of the whisky in his story. The joke was just as good with Tartan Label as with Black and White. So Melvin changed the name, kept the joke, and received his cheque every week and his case every month.

Time passed and Melvin altered his act. The whisky joke dropped out of his repertoire. But the cheque and the case still arrived regularly, and every time Melvin had occasion to mention whisky on the stage, he said Tartan Label.

One night a card was handed into his dressing-room. It was the whisky representative. On the card was a note to say that he was in to see the first house and would be round at the interval. So Melvin hastily introduced the old whisky joke into his act in the first house.

The whisky man looked rather crestfallen when he came round. 'I see you're still mentioning Tartan Label,' he said. 'Oh, yes,' answered G.S. Melvin.

The whisky man cleared his throat. 'Well, Mr Melvin,' he said, 'the old firm aren't doing so well just now. We've got to do a bit of retrenching. We are very grateful to you for having helped us so much, but we'll have to stop the present arrangement.'

'That's all right,' said Melvin. 'The joke was getting a bit over-worked anyway. But I tell you what. As long as I mention whisky, I'll keep on saying Tartan Label.'

'Good,' said the whisky man, much relieved, 'and, though we'll have to stop paying you the cheque, we'll continue to send you the case each month.'

And Melvin got a case of Tartan Label every month until the firm went out of existence.

Dave Bruce told me another Melvin story. Bruce was engaged to understudy Melvin in his Theatre Royal pantomime. The two comics met and G.S. Melvin studied Dave Bruce closely. 'Yes,' he said, 'you've got the right looks and the right build, but you'll never get a shot.' Melvin was right.

It might be said, mind you, that Harry Gordon did his bit of advertising too. When he was running his Beach Pavilion in Aberdeen, it was seriously stated by officials of Aberdeen Town Council that Harry Gordon was one of the chief advertisements for Aberdeen as a holiday resort.

Harry Gordon was yet another example of the boy who longs to get on to the stage. When he left school in Aberdeen, he became office boy with a firm of grain merchants there. He spent all his spare time appearing in concerts. He didn't care what kind of concert it was. After a year and a half as an office boy, Harry Gordon got the opportunity to go on the stage professionally. He was eighteen when he was offered a job in Monty's Pierrots at Stonehaven, which is not far from Aberdeen.

This resulted in an engagement at the Beach Pavilion in Aberdeen, a big step up. That was in 1913 and his salary was £2 a week. He joined the Army when the First World War broke out and spent three years in the Forces. Back to the Beach Pavilion he went as soon as he was demobilised and, apart from the war period, he spent 24 years at the one place, which may well be a record.

He graduated from entertainer to boss of the Pavilion in 1924 and then ran it until the Second World War closed it down in 1940. Gordon made the Beach Pavilion, Aberdeen, one of the principal dates for English stage stars. His list of guest artists reads like a collection of London Palladium bills.

Harry Gordon not only made the Beach Pavilion. He created a village whose fame spread so far that the Post Office were plagued the year round with letters addressed to the imaginary clachan of Inversnecky. The Post Office wasted no time with these letters. They sent them straight to Harry Gordon.

Many people, when they discovered there was really no such place as Inversnecky, decided to go to Aberdeen instead. That was why Harry Gordon was described as one of Aberdeen's chief advertisements.

Yet Inversnecky happened more or less by accident. There was a chorus girl at the Beach Pavilion who was always describing people as 'just sneckin' along'. She meant they were just dauner-ing.

One night on the Pavilion stage Harry Gordon wanted a funny name for a town. Out of the blue the chorus girl's favourite verb came to him, and he said, 'That was when I was in Inversnecky.' There was a roar of laughter, and so Inversnecky was born. It was to become a household word, even among people who had never been nearer Scotland than the Caledonian Market.

When Harry Gordon was on holiday in Spain, he went one evening to a night club in Barcelona. He saw a dark-looking chap sitting in a corner staring at him. The comedian got nervous, espec-cially when the dark-looking chap rose and strolled across to his table. He leaned over the table and said, 'Are you Inversnecky?' It turned out that the dark-looking chap was an Aberdonian too.

Like any other cult, Inversnecky-ism had its drawbacks, as Harry Gordon discovered when he was engaged to appear at the London Palladium. This was, of course, a great compliment to the comedian, and his local supporters went slightly daft about it. They hired a special train to take them from Aberdeen to London, because they wanted to be there to greet their favourite when he made his metropolitan debut.

The 'Inversnecky Special' caused a sensation. So did the Inver-snecky supporters when they appeared in the Palladium. They gave Gordon a great reception. But this had the opposite effect of the one desired. The London audience (like any other) preferred to judge for themselves. So Harry Gordon did not go down as well as he deserved. Soon after that the Marx Brothers flopped com-pletely at the London Palladium, so Harry Gordon could have said that he was in good company.

In any case, when he got back to Aberdeen, there was a letter waiting for him by a man who wrote that he was about to get mar-ried. Would Harry Gordon please let him know where he was appearing in the second week of June, because he wanted to go there for his honeymoon!

Apart from his stage work, Gordon made a tremendous impres-sion on radio audiences. Television was very late in arriving in Scotland, owing mainly to the war, so radio was the great commu-nicator in Scotland and, for that matter, a great deal of England.

Strangely enough, Scotch comics as a whole did not take to radio broadcasting well. It appeared that most of them needed the stimulus of an audience in a theatre. But Harry Gordon took to radio immediately and the time came when thousands of Sassenachs who had never seen him knew the voice of Harry Gordon as well as they knew the voice of Tommy Handley.

Pantomime was his métier, of course. After Will Fyffe died, Gordon had to team with another Scotch comic. In 1954 he had a great success in *Dick Whittington* in which his fellow comedian was Jack Radcliffe.

In those days Howard and Wyndham switched their pantomimes between Glasgow and Edinburgh. *Dick Whittington* had been produced in Edinburgh, so it was to be the pantomime at the Theatre Royal, Glasgow, in the 1955 season. Harry Gordon had been unwell for some time, but he refused to give up. He was rehearsing *Dick Whittington* in the run-up to the Theatre Royal opening when he died suddenly of a heart attack.

It was so near the opening that the Theatre Royal management were put in a perilous situation. They had to get a comic to play opposite Jack Radcliffe at very short notice indeed. The choice was severely limited, since most well-known Scotch comics were already engaged for the pantomime season.

They were fortunate enough to discover that another East Coast comic, Andy Stewart, though not free, was able to be persuaded to take over the Harry Gordon part. The worry was that Andy Stewart was a young man and was being asked to replace a mature comic.

But there was no alternative. Andy Stewart and Jack Radcliffe worked together at top pitch during the comparatively few days before the opening night. Apart from anything else, all the elaborate costumes had been designed for Harry Gordon, who was a buirdly chiel. Andy Stewart was a slim young man and a great deal of the pre-pantomime work was concerned with getting the costumes to fit him.

With all these troubles, it's not surprising that Andy Stewart, at the start of the run, was still seeking his way, although he kept on improving. He was nobly backed by Jack Radcliffe, a man whose aim was to be the complete professional and wanted to have complete professionals beside him.

As a pantomime critic for the newspapers in those days, I was determined to be truthful, but I had to have some compassion as well, especially in the unusual circumstances of this particular pantomime. So I let Andy Stewart down lightly, despite a certain youthful brashness which did not go at all with the part.

Andy Stewart must have learned a great deal from the run of *Dick Whittington*, especially under the tutelage of Jack Radcliffe. Although the theatrical powers-that-be were not over-impressed by his performance, they nevertheless recognised the difficulties under which he was working and after that he had never any difficulty in securing valuable theatrical contracts.

The change in his life was remarkable. He had, until this Glasgow Theatre Royal experience, been a comparatively minor comic, known principally for his work on radio. Before that he had been a student at the Royal Scottish Academy of Music and Drama in Glasgow, where he did not get on well with his teachers. He was an excellent mimic, which was perhaps not what they wanted, but he made a big hit in the Glasgow student revue, *College Pudding*. He suddenly left the Academy and no tears were shed.

I first saw him on the professional stage when he joined the repertory company at the old Metropole in Stockwell Street. He was appearing in that doddery old melodrama, *The Black Sheep of the Family*. Andy, of course, was the black sheep. In order to use his talent for mimicry, Harold Dayne, the producer, had inserted a scene in a night club, which was supposed to show the depths to which the Black Sheep had sunk.

Andy wasn't at that time much of an actor, but his night club scene was excellent. He was not overwhelmed with theatre offers but found a niche in BBC radio. With a regular series he did very nicely, and the listening public soon took him to their hearts.

I was in Aberdeen on journalistic business when I saw that Andy Stewart was appearing at the Tivoli Theatre. I went to see him and we adjourned to one of the Aberdeen seafront pubs. When I asked him about his future he said he had more or less given up the stage. He was concentrating on radio work from now on.

One afternoon he was rehearsing in the Glasgow studios of the BBC when there was one of those long hold-ups that seemed endemic in broadcasting in those days. Suddenly an idea came to him for a song. He was very keen on the old pipe tune, 'The Green Hills of Tyrol'. Sitting in the studio he worked out the lyrics of 'A Scottish Soldier' to the pipe tune.

When broadcast it was an instant success, not only in Scotland but in every country where there were Scots. It made Andy Stewart's name international. This was especially interesting because the tune was international too. The British Army pipe major who 'composed' it, took as his inspiration music which he had heard played by a Sardinian band during the Crimean War. It was actually the ballet music from Rossini's *William Tell.*

Andy Stewart's professional life was changed almost overnight, just as Will Fyffe's had been with 'I Belong to Glasgow'. He toured Canada and the USA with something of the same success as Harry Lauder. At the Empire in Glasgow his success vied with that of some of the biggest American stars.

Indeed, it's ironic that, when the Empire was no longer profitable and the decision was made to close it down, Andy Stewart's *White Heather Show* was chosen to be a farewell to a Glasgow music hall which had seen great days. It was packed every night for four weeks.

Unfortunately, Andy Stewart's health began to fail. Sometimes tours had to be shortened or even cancelled. He kept on bouncing back and you couldn't tell any difference in him. Indeed, the last time I saw him he seemed in the very bloom of health. It was an enormous charity concert held in the Theatre Royal, in the full splendour of its Scottish Opera transformation. All the well-known music hall names in Scotland appeared to be there. They had strict instructions to keep their acts down to a maximum of nine minutes.

Andy Stewart came on late in the programme. He appeared in one of his well-known characters, the old Aberdonian with a much-worn baggy suit and a wealth of Aberdeen wit. He was — there is no other word for it — terrific. He didn't worry about the set time limit. He held the stage for sixteen minutes, which was just about right because he was twice as good as anyone else who had appeared.

Now he has, officially, retired. Everyone who knows Andy Stewart wishes him well. Maybe they'll put up a plaque to him some day in the Royal Scottish College of Music and Drama!

And what of Jack Radcliffe, who nurtured Andy Stewart's first appearance in pantomime? He was an extraordinary Scotch comic who started as a 'tough' man in the music hall world and ended up as one of the most sophisticated comedians ever seen in Scotland.

Jack Radcliffe was born in Cleland, near the strangely named village of Omoa. But when he was two, he was taken to Bellshill, so he looked on himself as a Bellshill boy. His mother never left Bellshill and never saw her son on the stage.

Jack was brought up as a Baptist, which sounded strange for a man who was later known as Scotland's William Powell. For a time he was known as the Bellshill Boy Preacher. He travelled all over

Scotland with the Bellshill Baptist Church Male Voice Choir. He came from a singing family and had a fine voice.

His first appearance on any stage was in the title role of a kinderspiel — *Bobby Barefeet*. He was most enthusiastic about his part, especially when he found it included the lines:

A.B. Buff,
Gi'e the maister a cuff.
Gi'e him yin, gi'e him twa,
Knock his heid against the wa'.

Jack's father attended the kinderspiel and was horrified to see his son capering about the stage in his bare feet. Not only that, but Jack's feet were dirty. So Jack got a leathering from his father for appearing with his feet in that condition. Jack did his best to explain that it was all in character. Artistic verisimilitude was no excuse.

Besides singing for the Bellshill Baptist Male Voice Choir, Jack appeared at local concerts all over the district. He left school to become an electrical engineer, but didn't finish his apprenticeship. For a time he carried the monkey (the hod) for some bricklayers. He sawed wood in a sawmill. He worked down the pit and above the pit, and was engaged on machinery maintenance at a Lanarkshire pit when the General Strike of 1926 took place.

About this time Jack was interested in a concert party in Bellshill. They called themselves the Meritests, after a crossword puzzle competition which was popular at that time. Their manager was Tec White, the Scottish international footballer. Airdrie Hippodrome suddenly found itself without an attraction for the first week of the General Strike. Martin and Holbein were supposed to be bringing a revue to Airdrie, but they were far, far away and could get no transport.

The Meritests were engaged for the week at a fee of £16. There were seven Meritests but, when Jack got the £16 at the end of the week, he was so pleased that he tipped the stage manager £2. This at least shows aristocratic tendencies.

All Airdrie records were broken by the Meritests, but Jack thought that was because Airdrie people couldn't get into Glasgow because of the strike. At any rate, the Meritests were booked for a week at the Palace Theatre, Kilmarnock. The General Strike was still on, and the Meritests were faced with the difficulty of getting from Bellshill to Kilmarnock. Jack wasn't stumped. He went to a local ice-cream merchant and hired an ice-cream van for the journey. The seven Meritests packed themselves among the pokes

Jack Radcliffe
(SCOTTISH THEATRE ARCHIVES)

and went to Kilmarnock. They were inspired by the fact that their fee had been raised to £30 for the week.

For the first half of the show, the Meritests wore pierrot costumes. They were a great hit with the Kilmarnock folk. Jack played his fiddle and sang 'Trumpeter, what are you sounding now?' He was a riot. At the interval the Meritests changed for what they called the Road Show part of their programme. Jack put red on his nose and a funny kilt round his waist. 'I'll paralyse them,' he said.

Paralysis was on the programme all right, but it was the audience who paralysed Jack. The moment he appeared as a comic, they started to boo and shout. The manager of the theatre got so worried that he rang down the curtain and told the Meritests to get out. Then he put on a film and the audience quietened down.

The despondent Meritests went out to their ice-cream van to find a polis standing beside it. The polis said they had transgressed the Kilmarnock parking laws, but he would let them off if they got out of town at once. The ice-cream van broke down several times on the Fenwick Moor, and the Meritests didn't get back to Bellshill until 7 a.m. They'd expected to be back by midnight at the latest.

When Jack Radcliffe went along to the pit where he worked, he found he'd got the sack. He should have been on duty all night. So he was faced with going on the dole or on the stage. He decided an actor's life was the life for him. He is probably the only man who has been booed on to the stage.

Jack became a stooge to almost every comic in Scotland. That's why he decided, when he became a principal comic in later years, never to have a straight man working with him. Instead he persuaded a straight woman, Helen Norman, to join him in his act.

He got out of stooging when he helped to form a concert party which toured the Highlands. He was billed as 'Jack Radcliffe, Scotland's Greatest Comedian'. Like the rest of the company, Jack went round each town or village they came to with handbills. In one village he arrived at a charming old cottage. The door was open (as was the general custom in Highland clachans) so Jack stepped inside and laid one of his handbills on the hallstand. Just then an old lady appeared, saw Jack and the handbill and insisted on his waiting while she read it.

When the old lady came to 'Jack Radcliffe, Scotland's Greatest Comedian', her eyebrows went up and she said, 'I always thought Scotland's greatest comedian was Harry Lauder.' Jack was not nonplussed. 'Madam', he said, 'every comic in this country thinks he's Scotland's greatest comedian.' He then withdrew.

Eventually he arrived at the Empress Theatre at St George's Cross, Glasgow (much later to become Jimmy Logan's New Metropole) and met Harold Dayne. The former actor in Charlie Denville's transpontine drama company was known as a reliable stage teacher and helped several Scotch comics to some standard of success.

After Dayne's training, Jack Radcliffe's motto was, 'If you can't make them laugh, make them cry.' Consequently, he cut funny songs completely out of his act. Jack was acutely audience-conscious. He was always saying things to the audience and even challenging people to fight. He was appearing at Birkenhead in a revue called *Spring Revels*, but he challenged the audience so many times that the management changed the title on the bills to the well-known fighting invitation, *Any Time You Like!*

Gradually Jack went up in the music hall world, so far that he and Helen Norman were invited to take part in a Royal Command Performance in London. This was an honour seldom conferred on Scottish music hall artists, and there was great interest in the inevitable BBC broadcast of the show.

Jack Radcliffe elected to do one of his old men character studies, of the type which Harold Dayne had encouraged him in. He had an exceptional gift for make-up and was a convincing dodderer on the stage. In this sketch he was a geriatric in the country and his minder was Helen Norman. They were discussing life around them, when Nellie mentioned picnicers.

Jack, of course, confused this with pink knickers and made a slightly rude joke out of it. It's the sort of thing which would be accepted as completely normal today. But in those days it was regarded as dreadful, particularly in front of the Royals. Nobody in Glasgow then could possibly have imagined the emergence of a Billy Connolly.

His career went into the doldrums for a while and the best he could do in pantomime was a season at the Metropole. He was still doing a somewhat truculent act, all the more because of criticism, and I recall that pantomime not so much for the comedy as one of the greatest cues for song that I have ever heard. The show was *Robinson Crusoe* and at one point our hero entered with a couple of Borzoi dogs, which were very popular then. She was greeted by the Demon King who uttered some nasty threats, at which she loosed the Borzois and they chased the Demon King off the stage. (They were, actually, his pet dogs.)

Robinson Crusoe turned round triumphantly to the audience and spoke these immortal words:

Vice will be vanquished, virtue will prevail,
Even if I have to take the 'Oregon Trail'.

She then sang 'The Oregon Trail'. It's occasions like this which make me feel that pantomime is a Scottish art form well worth preserving.

Gradually Jack Radcliffe was forgiven for talking about pink knickers and he came back to the top theatres in Scotland. His return was triumphant when he teamed up with Jimmy Logan in the sophisticated revues, *Half Past Eight*, at the Theatre Royal and the Alhambra.

I thought at the time that Jimmy Logan had aspirations to being the new Jack Buchanan, for he was very fond of the white tie and tails appearance. Jack Radcliffe, who had never been known as a dressy comedian, took to white tie and tails as if he'd worn them all his life. In fact, he became a real man-about-town, though he could still act the geriatric on the stage.

He was already the polished professional when he helped the young Andy Stewart to take over the Harry Gordon in *Dick Whittington*. He remained the polished professional right up to the end. He had made as fine a come-back as Tommy Lorne, but lived much longer to enjoy it.

SIX

THE GLASGOW BOYS

WHEN I STARTED THIS strange, eventful history, it took me some considerable time to get Harry Lauder out of my system. I find it rather the same with Tommy Lorne. I suppose it's the genius that does it. At any rate, Lorne had a strong, personal effect on several Glasgow comics, but in particular on George West and Dave Willis, both heroes of Glasgow music hall and pantomime in their day.

Tommy Lorne and George West were boyhood pals. They ran about the New City Road district of Glasgow together. Their Mecca was the Grand Theatre in the Cowcaddens, where there was an amateur night every Saturday. Here a brave boy could make a regular 9d.

The system of the Grand was simple. If you got the bird, you got 9d. George West said it wasn't difficult to get the bird, especially if you were well known. As the patrons went in, they bought four clay pipes at four a penny from an old man at the door. Each patron broke his clay pipes in four pieces. That was his ammunition. The bowl was one piece and was reserved for turns which, in the opinion of the patrons, rated a special bird.

Almost every Saturday, Tommy Lorne and George West appeared at the Grand and made their 9d each. One week Tommy suggested to George that they should join forces and do a play. He said they would present that famous drama, *Wee Curley, the Crossing Sweeper*, and he would be the Toff and George would be Wee Curley.

There was no script. All George knew he had to do was to go on with a brush, say he was Wee Curley, lie down to die in the snow, and then Tommy the Toff would come on and rescue him.

George made a successful entrance, because he borrowed the stage-wide brush that one of the stage-hands used to sweep the broken clay pipes off the stage. He lay down to die, and the patrons provided the snow in the form of bits of clay pipe.

While he was lying on the stage, George West could see Tommy Lorne arguing with the manager in the wings. Then he saw Tommy put on the manager's hat and stride on to the stage, Toffy like. Just as Tommy made his opening speech, 'Ah, a poor cross-ing-sweeper lying in the snow', somebody threw a potato.

The potato missed Tommy and hit the manager's hat fair and square. Tommy and George didn't wait for their 9d each. They legged it out of the Grand and never appeared at an amateur night there again. Tommy, as I have already revealed, went into the office of Blochairn Steelworks, but spent all his spare time learning to dance. George joined a lawyer's office and appeared for clients in the Small Debt Court in Glasgow.

Clog-dancing was all the rage at that time, and George West went in for competitions as a clog-dancer. He saw comedians doing well on the stage and wondered why he should knock his pan out in clog-dancing. He entered for an amateur competition, sang a comic song and won the first prize. He also got a contract for thir-teen performances at what he thought was £10.

Too late he discovered the figure was 10/-. Travelling expenses came to 15/-. All the same, that was the start of his professional career. After that he decided to be an imitator. He bought a cabinet filled with electric lights and hung a sword inside it, along with some clothes.

Then he imitated comics he had never seen and was a decided success. 'You should have heard me doing the late George Formby in a Glasgow accent,' George said to me with a shake of the head. (This, of course, was the original George Formby, who was dying of consumption on the stage and whose running gag was, 'Coughing well tonight'.)

He never did anything with the sword in his cabinet. That was just to make his act look good.

He started his pantomime career in *Cinderella* at Hartlepool. The manager of the show hadn't enough money to hire ponies to draw Cinderella's coach, so he got goats instead. Though the manager gilded their horns, the goats were not a success. That was the first and last time George ever appeared with goats.

In 1924 George West started his career as Princess's panto-mime comic in Glasgow, following his friend Tommy Lorne, who had left the Princess's for the Pavilion two years earlier. Along with the pantomime, West held a world's record. It's dangerous to claim records, but I cannot recall any other comedian who has ever made so many consecutive appearances (21) in one theatre.

James Bridie, the Glasgow playwright, described West as a great clown in the French tradition. He wore what amounted to a clown's make-up, usually with a 'fright' wig, and elaborately funny clothes. His last pantomime at the Royal Princess's Theatre in the Gorbals was the 1944-45 season. It was after that when Harry McKelvie surprised everyone by leasing it to the Glasgow Citizens' Theatre at a peppercorn rent.

George West was not the least surprised. He'd thought that he was in with the bricks. If fact, he was hoping that McKelvie would follow the tradition of his predecessor, Rich Waldon, who made a present of the theatre to his former page boy. But McKelvie was unpredictable, as I have demonstrated already.

Not that this affected West's career. He was immediately invited to sign up for the Theatre Royal pantomime, which had been having comedian problems ever since Tommy Lorne died. Under the aegis of Howard and Wyndham he modified his make-up and his costume and yet retained his popularity. He also retained his friendship with Harry McKelvie and almost every year he and his wife were invited to be the guests of the McKelvies on holiday tours to various parts of the world. I have been told that he still nourished hopes that the Princess's theatre would eventu-ally become his.

It was not to be, and it remains the Glasgow Citizens' to this day. They still have a pantomime every year, an immensely popular one, but I doubt if George West would have recognised it as a pan-tomime. He died some years ago in 'reduced circumstances'.

Tommy Lorne, not only put George West on to a stage career, but also had a considerable influence in developing the stage life of Dave Willis, a Glasgow comic who was unsurpassed in his own way. I have described how Lorne was lured from the Princess's pantomime to the Pavilion one. The entrepreneur who accom-plished this was named Elkan Simons.

He found Tommy Lorne such a valuable property that he sug-gested partnership. So the firm of Tommy Lorne and Elkan Simons Ltd was formed. It not only ran Tommy Lorne shows, but also put smaller shows on the road. It was the day of touring revues

George West with members of the cast of *Sunny Days*
at the Pavilion, Largs, early 1930s.
(H. KEMP HOLDINGS/SCOTTISH FILM ARCHIVE)

and Tommy Lorne, looking for talent, had seen a minor comedian he thought had promise. His stage name was Dave Willis and he was in the Glasgow mould. He was engaged for a Tommy Lorne and Elkan Simons revue called *Larks* at a salary of £25 a week. The year was 1931 and that was not bad money in those days. They even got as far afield as Huddersfield, according to a salary list for the revue that I have seen.

David Williams was born and brought up in the same part of Glasgow as Tommy Lorne and George West, near what used to be St George's Cross. His father was a butcher and, in his spare time, trainer to the West of Scotland Harriers. Young David was a bit of a harrier himself and once ran in a race with the famous Applegarth. He became an apprentice engineer and was popular for singing funny songs at works' concerts. The First World War sent Dave into the Royal Flying Corps. He was stationed at Winchester, where his unit started a concert party called the Radio Lights.

By this time Dave was married and had a small son. (That son was in the Royal Artillery in the Second World War. He later became the comedian Denny Willis.) Every time the baby saw an aeroplane he thought his father was in it and he'd shout, 'Daddy, daddy — 'way up a 'ky!' One night on the stage Dave imitated his son's cry and got a big laugh. He used the phrase quite a lot, but never imagined that this baby talk would one day go right round the world.

Engineer Willis, demobilised, found there was little or no engineering for him. He was on the dole for a whole year and during that time he joined an amateur concert party and met a lad called Frank Richards. They formed a double act and got their first professional date at the Casino Picture House in Townhead, Glasgow. There they were seen by an agent who got them a year's engagements.

Double acts on the stage have, generally, a habit of splitting. Willis and Richards went the way of all flesh. Frank Richards became one of George West's feeds in the Princess's pantomime. On his own Dave Willis went into a revue called *Scotch Broth* as second comic. Willis was essentially a visual comedian. He had only to run on to the stage to set the house in a roar. At one town in England he entered with his customary success. But the moment he started to speak, the audience shut up tight. He gagged and sang with growing desperation, but not a cheep came from them.

Next day the crestfallen comic was talking to the man who owned the garage opposite the theatre. 'What's wrong with me?' he asked. 'You're Scotch', replied the garage man. 'There are fifteen mills round this town, and in every single one of them all the managers and foremen are Scotch. D'you think these people are going to laugh at a Scotsman? Not so-and-so likely!'

Of all the songs that Dave Willis sang, by far the most popular was 'My Wee Gas Mask' when he appeared as 'the nicest looking warden in the ARP'. He made a record of the number which brought royalties from India and tributes from Canada. A Canadian newspaper printed the words of the chorus and said, 'This is the spirit of the British people.'

When he did this song on the stage, Dave produced all sorts of ridiculous things from his gas-mask container. But when he did it in a 'Happidrome' broadcast programme at a time when gas-masks had to be kept always at the ready, the BBC asked him to make it plain to the audience that he was only being funny. So Dave took out the ridiculous objects as usual, and then gave the audience a pep talk on not following his example.

Although it would be exaggerating to say that Dave Willis swept the Deep South, he was at least well known down there. He made three film comedies in England. He did a couple of weeks at the London Pavilion. And he was an enormous success at Liverpool in the last pantomime of the Second World War.

He was a comedian who was very jealous of his reputation and, as 'boss' of the pantomime, was complete dictator. I remember going to visit him behind the scenes when his dressing-room door

Dave Willis, in typical pose.
(H. KEMP HOLDINGS/SCOTTISH FILM ARCHIVE)

suddenly opened and out came the principal boy in a flood of tears. Dave had thought she was upstaging him.

Towards the end of Tommy Lorne's career both he and Dave Willis were appearing in Glasgow pantomimes at the same time. A big charity ball was arranged at the Piccadilly Club in Sauchiehall Street in aid of the Press Fund and both comedians agreed to appear in the All Star Cabaret at midnight.

I was on the Press Fund committee and I still recall the unexpected stramash which occurred when the order of the programme was being arranged on the spot. Dave Willis discovered that he was to follow Tommy Lorne. He refused at once and said he would leave the club there and then.

Somewhat timidly, a committee deputation went to see Tommy Lorne and explained the situation. Tommy just laughed. 'Ach, that's all right,' he said. 'Let the young man have his way.'

Dave went from success to success, being even more popular in Edinburgh than in his native Glasgow. He decided to retire while he was still at the top and followed the primrose path that so many comics have taken — he bought a hotel. It was right on the promenade at Rothesay, not far from the pier and it was one of the biggest on the Isle of Bute.

He invited me down for a day to see his new acquisition. It was in early Spring before the tourist season started, so I was not surprised to find the hotel very quiet. What did surprise me, though, was when Dave took me into the cocktail bar for a drink and I saw the two white-jacketed barmen smoking. Nor did they stop smoking while we were there. Dave didn't seem to notice anything wrong.

He called the manageress to take us on a short tour of the hotel and it seemed to me by the look on his face that Dave was seeing some parts of his property for the first time. Then up we went to the very fine suite he occupied with his wife. In the sitting room I was surprised to see a couple of artist's easels.

'This is our favourite hobby now,' he explained. 'The wife and I both paint scenes of Rothesay and other places on the island. We get picture postcards and copy them. Ever tried it? It's very interesting.' I took his word for it.

Later in the day Dave and I had a stroll along the promenade and he was constantly greeted by the natives. When I commented on this, he said, 'Oh, aye, it's always like this. In fact, there's some talk of making me Provost of Rothesay one of these days.'

Dave Willis never became Provost of Rothesay. The next we

heard was that the hotel had failed and Dave had lost all his money. He and his wife came back to Glasgow and took a small flat in a tenement at Anniesland Cross. I went to see them there and Dave was certainly making the best of it. 'I'm doing not so badly,' he said. 'I never realised there was money in these Sunday night concerts. I get one most Sundays and that keeps us going all right.'

The last time I saw him was in the Gateway Theatre in Edinburgh (now a studio for Scottish Television). An Edinburgh man had written a play about the life of a Scotch comic and Dave was asked to appear as the lead. He did his best but it was obvious that he had difficulty in remembering his words. At the interval I saw the unfortunate author sitting with his head in his hands. The run was mercifully short.

Dave Willis and his wife went to Peebles, where he had a severe stroke and died. You can still see traces of the Dave Willis style in the work of his son, Denny — though Denny is much taller than his father was and does not try to copy him. I suppose it shows that a sort of comic genius is still being carried on. And it's notable that Denny Willis is even more popular in European theatres than he is in this country. But if there is a hidden moral in all this, I must admit it eludes me.

Dave Willis differed from Harry Lauder in that Lauder pretended to be 'mean' and was generous in private. Dave really did watch the pennies. He was particularly parsimonious when it came to paying song writers. His idea of a reasonable price for a song was £2. The only song-writer he was comparatively generous to was the retired comic, Wullie Lindsay, who wrote most of the best Willis numbers. He usually got £5.

Wullie Lindsay was one of the great characters of the Glasgow music hall. He was a very good friend of mine (or maybe I should say I was a very good friend of his!). He was a very funny man and he was doing well on the music hall scene. He was engaged as lead comic for the summer season at Dunoon, which was one of the top dates on the Firth of Clyde. Those were the days when Glaswegians flocked to the Clyde coast for their holidays and knew nothing of Spain except that it was a country somewhere in Europe which sent us oranges.

One afternoon during the run Wullie decided to take the steamer across to Gourock, where he had friends working in the big show at the Cragburn Pavilion. As he crossed the main street he was run down by a car. He was taken to hospital with a badly broken leg and the Dunoon management had to make frantic efforts to replace him for the rest of the season.

It's maybe not surprising that he turned to the solace of alcohol after that and theatrical engagements became fewer because he was not considered to be reliable. Every now and then he would fail to turn up for a show. So he turned to song and gag writing. Harry Ashton of the King's thought that Wullie had the finest collection of gag books in Britain.

He was not above rather questionable methods to acquire them. In a Glasgow library he discovered an authoritative American treatise on the philosophy of theatre gags. It was wonderful stuff and Wullie thought out a plan. He went back to the library and confessed that he had been reading the book beside the fire, nodded off to sleep and it had fallen into the fire. The librarian admonished him for his carelessness and fined him 7s 6d. Wullie paid the fine and cherished the book for ever more.

Writing songs and gags became his first interest and a main source of income but he was also interested in conjuring, juggling, shadowgraphy and paper-tearing. He was possibly the finest paper-tearer in Scotland. He was an expert on make-up and there was a notable occasion when a Glasgow editor got into a fight one night and wanted repairs done to his face before he reappeared in his newspaper office next morning. I had introduced him to Wullie in a pub and he asked me to get Wullie and his make-up box to him as soon as possible.

This was done and Wullie went to work. I didn't see the result myself but the editor thought it was a great success. If the word of Wullie's wizardry had gone round the Glasgow newspaper offices, he might well have had an entirely new career open to him.

But Wullie was a wayward genius. Song-writing was a great idea, because new comic songs were always wanted and the payment was immediate. One night he was in the Grimsby in Cambridge Street, Glasgow — a fish and chip shop extensively patronised by music hall artists and run by a chap from Grimsby. The proprietor pointed proudly to a new picture of Dave Willis on the wall. 'Look at that,' he said, 'he gets more like Hitler every day.'

Wullie Lindsay seized an empty chip bag and immediately wrote on the back of it the chorus of a big Dave Willis hit — 'I'm getting more like Hitler every day.' This was a great success until the Government banned imitations of Corporal Schicklgruber in the days before 3 September 1939, because they did not want to hurt the feelings of the leader of a friendly state.

I knew Wullie so well because he came to me with the idea of a new series when I was Features Editor of a Glasgow newspaper. It was more or less to write his life story, or the bits which could be printed, plus the Glasgow city knowledge he had acquired. It was arranged that we would meet (always in a pub) once a week and he would hand me his notes, then we'd discuss them and I would ghost the article under Wullie's name.

The series went down well, except that Wullie was occasionally worried by some of the words I used. Once he 'phoned me in great anxiety. 'Jack, you've got me in big trouble,' he said. 'Ma pals were readin' ma article. Whit the hell does "esoteric" mean?'

Indeed, the series was so successful that one of the other evening newspapers (there were three of them in Glasgow then) made Wullie an offer he couldn't refuse. So he went to the rival, where his new series lasted just five weeks. When we next met he was quite bewildered. 'Ah didnae realise,' he said, 'that Ah cannae write without you.'

I persevered in trying to help Wullie because I liked him so much. One difficulty was that, unless he had a week-end theatrical engagement, his habit was to buy on Saturday a bottle of red wine known popularly as 'Ra Lanny' in Glasgow, drink one glass out of it and fill the bottle up with brandy. He then spent Saturday and Sunday contemplating his navel.

Every now and then Wullie made a come-back. He got a week's engagement at the Empire Theatre and I went to his Monday night first-house performance, keeping my fingers crossed. I needn't have bothered. Wullie was assured, funny and popular. When I congratulated him at the end of his week, he said, 'Oh, Ah think Ah'm quids in there, Jack, Ah gave the stage manager a bottle o' whisky on the last night.' Strange to say, he was never asked back.

At James Bridie's instigation, the Citizens' Theatre had continued to run their own pantomimes and kept the Princess's tradition of 13-letter titles. They had their biggest success with *The Tintock Cup*, in which the chief comics were Duncan Macrae, Stanley Baxter and Molly Urquhart. It could have easily come up to the Harry McKelvie record for a run, but the Scottish Arts Council pointed out sternly that the theatre did not receive a grant for running pantomimes.

The Friends of the Citizens' Theatre had, apparently, read some of the Wullie Lindsay articles I had written and got in touch with me to ask if I could arrange for Wullie to give them a talk on music halls and pantomimes. He said he would and the response from the Friends was so great that they had to hire the banqueting hall of the Trades House in Glasgow to hold the number of people who had bought tickets.

Wullie put on his best suit — well, I mean his *other* suit — and told me that he wanted me to come on to the stage with him when invited so that he could show the audience that anybody could be a comic if he had a good stooge. He was to be the stooge and I was to be the comic.

That night, to put it simply, Wullie was wonderful. He couldn't put a word wrong. You'd have thought he'd been addressing big audiences for years. At the end he received an ovation. The Friends of the Citizens' Theatre agreed that they'd never had an evening like it.

Next day in the pub he said to me, 'That settles it. After last night Ah'm gaunna take up lecturing. Wi' the money Ah goat Ah'm buyin' a new suit.'

I wasn't quite sure how he was going to get lecture engagements, but I did a lot of lecturing myself at that time and I thought I'd look out for opportunities for Wullie to reveal his new talent. It turned out easier than I expected. I had a date to lecture at Barrie's birthplace, Kirriemuir. They had a strong Literary Society there. It was impossible for me to get back to Glasgow that night, so they put me up in a very pleasant hotel. The secretary came back to the hotel with me and asked if I could recommend any other speakers. Right away I told her about Wullie and his success with the Friends of the Citizens' Theatre. I gave her his address and a lecture was fixed. Wullie was full of the joys.

On the evening of Wullie's lecture I received an anxious telephone call. It was the secretary of the Kirriemuir Literary Society and she was asking where Wullie was. They had waited for an hour for him to arrive, and then the audience had to go home. I couldn't help. I didn't know where Wullie was and I couldn't reach him by 'phone because he didn't have one.

I never discovered what happened to Wullie that night. He didn't get in touch with me to explain and, in fact, I never saw him again. I had a three months' illness, then joined another newspaper. I'd like to have met him again but the nature of my new work prevented it. He gave me some of the best laughs and worst headaches I've ever had. Writers on the theatre in Glasgow have never mentioned him. As far as I'm concerned, I'll never forget him.

BRIGTON'S BIG BEENIE

MOST GLASGOW COMICS have been and still are doted upon by their fellow natives. There have been comedians who were the exception to this rule, but they are a very small minority. But I must pay a special tribute to one particular man — Tommy Morgan. To go round his native Brigton (Bridgeton to you) with him was a heart-warming experience. He was greeted everywhere by happy faces and hearty shouts. The point was that he was not just a local boy who'd made good — he was still one of them. Some of them had been to school with him and they were his especial chinas. (For the benefit of the uneducated, china is rhyming slang for mate — china plate = mate, see?)

When Tommy left school he had various jobs and was working in a Bridgeton chocolate factory when the First World War started in 1914. He immediately joined the army by pretending he was eighteen years of age when, actually, he was only sixteen. He was in France when he was seventeen. His father kept sending out a copy of Tommy's birth certificate to every one of Tommy's commanding officers in turn, so Tommy was always changing his regiment. He was in seven different regiments during 1914-1919.

While he was behind the lines in France he was personal orderly to Sir Douglas Haig for a spell. More important to his later life, he joined an Army concert party as stooge to Corporal Alf Vivian, who had been a London comedian before the war. Through the concert party he met such interesting visitors, who had come out to entertain the troops, as G.H. Elliott, Leslie Henson, Eric Blore and Randolph Sutton, and the stage got into his blood.

Since his uncle was a plater in a Clyde shipyard, Tommy was made a plater's helper when he was demobilised. He hated the work. He joined an amateur concert party in Glasgow called the Rockets and made a friend of a chap named Tommy Yorke who was a singer in the show. There were only five Rockets and they gave a two-hours' performance. Their first concert was in Govan and was such a success that they got a return date in a fortnight.

But a fortnight later only Morgan and Yorke turned up. They didn't like to disappoint the audience, so Tommy Morgan put some red on his nose and they gave the whole show themselves. They were so successful that they decided to turn professional.

Their first date was at a picture house in Kirkintilloch. The bill consisted of three acts and two pictures, and Yorke and Morgan were top of the bill. Tommy was so proud of this that he asked the manager for a copy of the bill, took it home and showed it to the family.

Yorke and Morgan had a hard road to hoe — 'One week in, ten weeks out,' he told me. Then Tommy Morgan lost his voice. When his voice came back, he carried on, but agents were scared of booking him in case he lost it altogether. Once they thought of giving the whole thing up. Morgan was on holiday when he got a wire from Yorke: 'Offered revue, £10. Shall I take it?' They took it.

They got, as I have mentioned, a small job in the Princess's pantomime of 1923-1924, when Harry McKelvie took the comics 'in bundles of six' and threw them on the stage. Then they joined an entrepreneur named Gordon Inglis in a pantomime called *Santa Claus* and never looked back. In 1931 Tommy Morgan went to the Metropole Theatre as chief comic for a pantomime season. Apart from brief visits to posher pantomimes in the Empire and Alhambra Theatres, he stayed for the rest of his professional life in Metropole pantomimes. Soon his life was to follow a definite pattern — winter and spring in pantomime at the Metropole, summer and autumn in his own show at the Pavilion.

Before this pattern emerged he appeared in music halls all over Scotland. I recall going out to the Hamilton Hippodrome (by tram-car!) to see him. And he was in a summer show in a tent at Portobello when he got word that the great C.B. Cochran was in the audience. The company expected Cochran to stay for half-an-hour or so, but the maestro waited the full three and a quarter hours until 'God Save the King'. Then he went round behind the backcloth to tell Tommy Morgan he was the funniest man he'd seen for twenty years.

Tommy was naturally pleased, but stage people have a habit of being ebullient and over-complimentary. Cochran, however, was so serious about it that he repeated the compliment in one of his books. For a year or two Tommy awaited the summons to London, but nothing ever happened. Not that it worried Morgan a great deal. He was soon doing so well that he was able to put on his own shows and theatrical people in Glasgow talked with awe of the money he was making.

I was lucky enough to see one of the Morgan shows in the lovely Opera House in Belfast. At the time I was writing the scripts for a BBC series called *Make It a Double*, the basis of which was the life and times of Scottish double acts. Eddie Fraser, the Glasgow man who nurtured Stanley Baxter, Jimmy Logan and a wheen of others, was the producer and, when it came to Morgan and Yorke, they were in Belfast and I had to fly there.

Scotch comics, and particularly Glasgow comics, have always been popular in Belfast but Tommy Morgan was outstandingly so. I spent the day talking to Yorke and Morgan and in the evening went along to the Opera House to see the show. Naturally, there wasn't a seat to be had, but that didn't worry me because I really wanted to see the audience.

I watched the show from the wings for a while and then I went up to the dress circle and watched the audience. As far as Morgan appearances were concerned, I thought that nothing could surpass the reception he got from Glasgow Pavilion audiences. I was wrong. Just in front of me was a line of Irish middle-aged women. Tommy was doing an act which I knew well and at every one of his cracks this whole line of women would rock backwards and forwards, screaming with laughter. When they did their backwards rock the long row of seats was almost wrenched out of its moorings. In fact, there was a crack from the seats every time there was a crack from the stage. I must admit I got quite alarmed, but the Irish have their own way of doing things and nobody else seemed to worry a bit.

Tommy Morgan's nickname was 'Clairty', which was odd because clairty in Glasgow means dirty and Morgan was anything but. Actually, he took the phrase from his mother who, when astonished by anything, would cry, 'Clare to goodness!' (Translation — 'I declare to goodness.') He used it as a gag once or twice, and then found that people in the street would say, 'There's Clairty away by.'

So he became Clairty. For a time he had a cabin cruiser named

Clairty. Once a letter was sent from England addressed merely to 'Clairty, Scotland'. It was delivered right away to Rothesay, where Tommy was appearing in a summer show. Even when Morgan went into the London Palladium one night to see the Crazy Gang from the stalls, people spotted him and were shouting 'Clairty, Clairty' all through the show.

Possibly Tommy Morgan's best known character was 'Big Beenie', a huge blonde, always in the latest fashion (which seldom suited her), and a man chaser who seldom caught up with her prey. She did eventually land an American soldier (this was during the war when, after the United States came in, Glasgow was packed with GI's who always landed at Greenock and made straight for the nearest city). So Tommy's creation became 'Big Beenie, the GI Bride' and there was a new adventure in every change of programme during the Pavilion run. It could have been said to be a kind of stage 'soap opera', but the term was unknown then.

Morgan was friendly with Press people, not because he was seeking publicity, but because he found an affinity with them. At the time I was working for the old Evening News in Hope Street and at least once a week Tommy would put his head round the door of my room and say, 'How about lunch?' We often went down to the oyster bar in Howard Street and swallowed a couple of dozen each, accompanied by draughts of Guinness.

Then Tommy started inviting my wife and me out for lunch on Sunday. My wife was a journalist too, and Tommy and his wife, Celie, would call for us at our flat in North Kelvinside (it was actually just a kick in the chin from Maryhill, but North Kelvinside was its official name). He ran a big car but did not drive himself. His driver was known as Mac and had been the regular taxi driver for Tommy before he got a car of his own.

So we'd go out for lunch. Tommy had a penchant for posh places and it could be Gleneagles or Turnberry or any one of the big caravanserai in our airt of Scotland. I have to admit that I found it embarrassing because Tommy insisted on being the host and the best I was allowed to do was to buy a round in the cocktail bar before we went into the dining room. Fortunately this practice lasted only one summer, which seems an ungracious way of putting it but was true.

In the middle of one of his summer seasons at the Pavilion, Tommy became too ill to appear on the stage, although he still managed to get to the theatre to supervise the production. He also succeeded in appearing in the Royal Variety Performance at the

Tommy Morgan in *Mother Goose* at the Metropole, 1939.
(GLASGOW HERALD)

Alhambra in the summer of 1958, when the audience were surprised to see that his hair had turned white. I didn't realise how ill he was until Eddie Fraser asked me to do an hour-long radio script on the great days of the Princess's pantomime. I suggested that we should include the one and only appearance there of Yorke and Morgan, which I've already described.

We got in touch with Tommy and to our surprise he said he thought that Tommy Yorke had still the original sketch of the three minutes which they were allowed to do. Tommy Yorke, indeed, had kept it and we felt it was worth including in the show as a tiny but genuine part of Glasgow's music hall history.

All was well until it came to the recording of Yorke and Morgan. Tommy was not able to come to the BBC studios in Queen Margaret Drive, so Eddie Fraser decided that the mountain must go to Mahomet. It was arranged that an Outside Broadcast unit should go to Kelvin Court, Glasgow's first group of luxury flats, and the sketch would be recorded in Tommy Morgan's sitting room.

The OB van was parked at the back of Kelvin Court and a line was run up to the Morgan flat. Tommy was all right in general conversation but when it came to the Princess's pantomime sketch he couldn't remember his lines. It was painful in the extreme to watch him searching vainly for the words and at one point he said bitterly, 'Ach, they should jist take me out an' shoot me!'

Eddie Fraser was patient and determined. Tommy Yorke would say his line and then there was a pause and Tommy Morgan had several tries at the response. After an hour and a half's work we had succeeded in getting all the words of the three minute sketch. Later at Broadcasting House, Glasgow, the lines were cobbled together and to any listener the sketch came over as bright and as fast as when it was originally done.

It was not long after that when Tommy Morgan died. He had just reached the age of sixty and should have had many more years in the theatre. I will always remember him for his generosity. He not only made his audiences happy but also spread the happiness to his cast, to young and aspiring comedians and to his many friends. A man can hardly have a better memorial than that.

A great many comics I have known have carefully safeguarded their own position, to the extent of getting rid of any competition in the cast. Morgan, on the contrary, looked for new comics and would engage them in his shows in the hope that they would emerge fully-fledged. Not only comics, of course, but any young act he admired.

Accordingly, he booked a girl singer he'd seen in Belfast, one of his favourite stamping grounds. Her name was Ruby Murray and she was completely unknown outside Northern Ireland. He kept on encouraging her until she became a star.

Likewise, he brought a couple of young Glasgow comics into his show and gave them opportunities they might never have had. They were Larry Marshall and Charlie Sim. Later they were to become two of the best known personalities in Scottish Television, through the daily programme, *The One O'Clock Gang*. It's more or less forgotten now, but it was an enormous favourite with Scottish viewers.

I recall a big success I had with a short programme on STV called *Whigmaleeries*. It was invented by the then chief of STV, Noel Stevenson, when the renewal, or otherwise, of STV's charter was to be considered after their first stint. It was, officially, a serious programme, though I didn't worry about that. It got record viewing figures for the simple reason that it followed immediately *The One O'Clock Gang* and most housewives in Scotland couldn't be bothered to switch to another channel. That's one reason why I seldom trust viewing or listening figures. And this especially applies to television, because so many people are inclined to leave the set on all day whether they are watching a programme or not.

I'm sorry to say that Charlie Sim, an engaging young man, has died. Larry Marshall, who changed his name from Tomasso because every time he answered the 'phone and gave his name, the caller would say 'Hello, Mr Marshall', had quite a career on the stage and on television before he found his perfect métier.

Larry's outstanding gift was his immense rapport with an audience. So he capitalised on that and for some years now has conducted a long running cabaret show in an Edinburgh hotel. It is packed out every night for the season and the avid audience is filled mainly with Americans, Canadians, and other Sassenachs. They get the whole Scotch works and enjoy every moment of them. It's odd that there are now several of these night shows in Edinburgh but, as far as I know, only one of them in Glasgow, and it isn't in a hotel.

Larry Marshall would be among the first to express his indebtedness to Tommy Morgan, but there's a long list of debtors. I recall one occasion when Tommy said to me, 'I've got a wonderful new comic for the next summer show at the Pavilion. I've signed him up for two years, but by that time he'll be so famous that he'll go somewhere else.'

I haven't often heard one comic say that about another and I went to the first night of the new Morgan show at the Pavilion with some reservations. I needn't have worried. Morgan's new signing was called Chic Murray. He appeared with his wife, Maidie, a small, lovely girl who played the accordion, while Chic, standing behind her, towered above her and made his inimitable comments. I could see what Tommy meant right away. Here was a complete original, who turned familiar words and phrases into something out of this world. I had never seen a Scotch comic remotely like him. And, of course, it came to pass as Tommy Morgan had forecast, that he went on to bigger, if not better, things.

We became friends, so much so that he stopped doing his act when we were together. But it surprised me when one day he asked me if I was willing to do a television commercial with him. I said 'yes' right away, and it turned out to be a voice over act, and a cartoon would be fitted to what we had said. Chic explained that the producers wanted to record it in Glasgow, but they had no facilities in any of the local studios. Could I suggest somewhere suitable?

Chic Murray and Maidie (GLASGOW HERALD)

The only place I could think of was the Glasgow Art Club in Bath Street, of which I was a member. I am still a member but, now that I am making this revelation, I may well be expelled. What happened was that I took Chic and the two visitors who were in charge of the recording into the Club as guests and we did the work in an unoccupied room.

Chic had said to me that there was to be either an outright fee or a payment on a royalty basis, according to how many showings the commercial received. The outright fee was £50 each (quite a lot of money at the time) and he proposed that we should accept that and waive the royalties.

I agreed, and we made several different versions of the script. The two recording chaps took the tapes away, and paid us there and then. I have never discovered whether this great work ever appeared on the tiny screen or not. Chic did become a cult figure in the music hall world, much as Billy Connolly is now. When he was in the money he and Maidie bought a hotel in Edinburgh and Maidie retired from the act to run it. This was one comic's hotel which prospered and it is still a popular place in Edinburgh, though Maidie has retired from management. At the moment she is helping a young author from East Kilbride to write Chic's life story.

The last time I met Chic was in the physiotherapy department at the Western Infirmary. I had slipped on the ice within yards of my home, dislocating my shoulder and also chipping my shoulder blade. Indeed, I am possibly the only man who can claim genuinely to have a chip on his shoulder. My youngest brother kindly gave me a lift to the Western and, as we entered the Casualty Department, who should be there but Chic Murray, with his arm in a sling.

I introduced my brother and asked Chic what had happened. He explained that he had been appearing in a film and one of the things he had to do was to walk a tightrope. With a wealth of detail he explained how he had been trained and become an expert on the wire. When it came to the filming of this incident he was rather disturbed when he discovered that the director had forgotten to tell him that, for some reason, the wire had been changed from a tight one to a slack one. It was too late for Chic to do anything about it so he started to cross and half way over he fell off. Hence his dislocated arm.

So vivid was Chic's description that my brother believed every word of it. Knowing Chic, I waited until we started physiotherapy together and asked him what had really happened. It turned out that he had slipped on the ice just as I had.

His last appearance was in a disastrous Hogmanay programme which was televised from Gleneagles Hotel. Everything that could go wrong seemed to go wrong that night. It was not long after that episode that Chic died suddenly, though I hasten to add that his death had nothing to do with the unfortunate television programme.

Tommy Morgan's successor in the Pavilion Summer Show was 'Sexy Lexie'. That's what Lex McLean liked to be called. He was one of the first Scotch comics to leave the straight and narrow path and indulge in the kind of comedy that Max Miller, the Cockney comedian, had made so popular. He had the same manner of looking at the audience with a slightly shocked expression after he had said something particularly outré.

To me he was a clown in the Grimaldi mould. You'll recall the famous story of Grimaldi who suffered from bouts of intense depression. When he went to see a doctor and explained his troubles, the doctor said, 'You need taking out of yourself. Why

Lex McLean (centre) with Walter Carr and Charlie Sim
(as the conductor) in his Glasgow corporation bus sketch.
(GLASGOW HERALD)

don't you go to the theatre and see Grimaldi?' It was not that Lex
suffered so much from depression as that he always gave me the
impression that he felt he was not getting the praise he deserved.
He said to me once, talking of one of the Glasgow newspaper critics, Mamie Crichton, 'All you've got to do to get into Mamie
Crichton's column is to carry a spear in something by Shake-
speare. She never says anything about the really good shows.' He
meant, of course, shows in which Lex McLean was appearing.

Lex did the normal training as a Scotch comic in the seaside
concert parties and the minor music halls. He had a guid conceit of
himself from an early age and annoyed some newspaper people
with his oft repeated claim that he was by far the best-equipped
comedian in Scotland. 'I can do everything,' he said with simple
modesty. Any man like that is bound to be sniped at occasionally.

But snipers were put in their place when he took over the Pavilion Summer Show after Tommy Morgan retired. He beat even
Morgan's records and then went on to one successful television
show after another. In television he used that fine actor, Walter
Carr, as his straight man and also had Larry Marshall, Charlie Sim
and John Mulvaney in his shows. John Mulvaney might have

become a top comic, for he had a pleasant style of his own. Unfortunately, he died young.

Walter Carr, of course, has become one of the leading pantomime dames in Scotland, though he is also a fine straight actor in the legitimate theatre. (I love that expression, 'legitimate' theatre because it has the obvious connotation that the music hall is a bastard art!) I first saw him in the Pitlochry Festival Theatre in the old days, when it was still a tent. Carr is a real theatre man and he has now reached the stage where he is regarded as a fount of all knowledge, and is called on to give advice and wise words to producers, directors and performers. Long may he reign.

Lex McLean kept reigning at the Pavilion. He bought a fine house on the front at Helensburgh, with beautiful views of the Firth of Clyde. This was very convenient from the travelling point of view. When he took his final curtain at the second house of his Pavilion show, he appeared in his ordinary clothes, unlike most performers. He timed the end of the show to perfection, so that all he had to do was to take a few minutes' walk to Queen Street Station and catch the Helensburgh train. Then a taxi would take him home and he was probably having his nightcap much earlier than some of his audience who lived in outlying parts of Glasgow.

I am not suggesting, by the way, that Lex McLean was an unhappy man. He was rich, had a charming wife and a good life style. Every show he was in was a riotous success. But I remember spending a day with him at Helensburgh and he was so out-of-key with the world that I wished, when I got back to Glasgow, that there was a Lex McLean show I could go to see and be cheered up.

Just like Tommy Morgan, Lex succumbed to a serious illness. The last time I saw him was just outside Broadcasting House, Glasgow. He had been recording a television programme there and, with some of the other performers, was making his way to one of the Byres Road pubs. I was going into the BBC myself and had no time to talk to him. But I still recall how worried I was at his appearance.

I made a point of finding out what the programme was and watching it on the appropriate night. There was Lex on the screen, as funny and bright as ever. I'm glad that my last memory of him was a pleasant one.

I can't think of anybody who has followed Lex McLean. I suppose the nearest would be Hector Nicol, who was perhaps a deeper shade of blue than Lex. He had his private troubles too but, like Lex, was invincibly determined to face them. Harry Lauder would have thought that Hector was not in the 'keep it clean' class, but Nicol had an engaging style that made him very popular. He was, of course, very strong on the club circuit, which was quite unknown in my young days. Sometimes today, I must confess, I feel that working in clubs is not conducive to good performances on the stage, unless the entertainer realises the difference and makes allowances for the new medium.

One comic who has completed the transfer successfully is Andy Cameron. He is a very intelligent man, even if he does support Rangers' Football Club. He also finds it possible to get away from the microphone now and then. I must admit that I find microphones an absolute blight. In the great days of my youth no stage performer needed a microphone. And yet they seldom shouted. The top comics had the trick of projecting their voices right back to the pit stalls and right up to the gallery.

We even had men like Whispering Jack Smith and Melville Gideon of the Co-Optimists who sang softly yet so clearly that every word was heard. Indeed, to hear Melville Gideon sing 'I'm tickled to death I'm single' was a treat that I remember to this day. I realise that I may appear a crusty old Colonel Blimp, far behind the times and maybe even afraid of the benefits of modern technology. Well, so be it. I really don't see many benefits myself but I try to remember what a top chef told me once.

I'd referred to some dish being 'as good as mother used to make' and he was distinctly displeased. 'What you have just eaten,' he said, 'is better than your mother could possibly have made. All this "like mother made" stuff just comes from your imagination.'

So perhaps I should stop my comparisons with the old days on the basis that they were better than today. I know there are fine things like Scottish Ballet and *The Three Estates* at the Edinburgh Festival and, occasionally but memorably, Citizens' Theatre productions in Glasgow. But there is not the feast of big productions from London that there used to be.

Do you realise that you'd hardly ever see the big musical shows of the type that was our regular fare forty or fifty years ago if it wasn't for the local amateur productions? Amateurs are the only people who can put on such shows as lavishly as those I was privileged to attend as a newspaper critic. And I must say that their standards of production are notably high. One good job that Glasgow District Council does is to continue the tradition of giving four weeks in the Spring and the same period in the Autumn for amateur productions in the King's Theatre.

EIGHT

THE FORGOTTEN THEATRE

NOW WE HAVE A 'sea-change into something rich and strange'. Just in case you don't recognise the immortal phrase of the Swan of Avon, I'll say it in pantomime terms. If you've seen *Aladdin and his Wonderful Lamp* you'll recollect that the wicked magician, Abanazar, performs all sorts of conjuring changes, so that sometimes you're not sure where you are. I'm about to accomplish one of these changes. From renowned Scottish music hall performers we're going to the places where they performed.

In these same places were seen some of the world's most famous actors and artistes and we must not be so parochial as to exclude them from this record. And so I am going to concentrate on the theatres I knew and what happened in them. I liked all the Glasgow theatres, but some more than others. And so I trust you won't think I am being perverse if I start with Glasgow's forgotten theatre, the Coliseum in Eglinton Street.

If I mention the Coliseum to any of my friends (except a few of my contemporaries), they say 'The what?' The Coliseum in its prime was the largest theatre in Glasgow and had the largest stage. Its only trouble was being the farthest South theatre in the city and there is a strange idea among those who live on the North Bank of the River Clyde that crossing the river to go anywhere is, to use an old Glasgow saying, a case of 'oot o' the warld and intae Polmadie'. I don't think I need to explain that, but Polmadie was traditionally a place which was seldom entered by citizens of Glasgow, except those who lived in Polmadie, of course.

The Coliseum still stands, large and neglected, and empty, of course, in a part of Glasgow which has been 'improved' by knocking down fine old tenements and sometimes putting nothing in their place. As I write, it has been in the news because of a suggestion that the Scottish National Orchestra, cribbed, cabined and confined in the comparatively small City Hall, should take the Coliseum over and make it into their new home.

Since, from an early age, I went to every pantomime in Glasgow, I recall seeing *Robinson Crusoe* at the Coliseum in the very early 'twenties. The Principal Boy was a popular singer named Fred Barnes. Male principal boys were unknown in Glasgow in those days, though I later saw Randolph Sutton as Boy in a pantomime at the Pavilion. However, Fred Barnes was known to be 'gay' (although we didn't denigrate that adjective in those days). The night I went to the Coliseum I was most impressed to see that the front two rows of the stalls were completely filled with his friends, who went into raptures over his every appearance.

After all these years I still remember his big 'hit' song.

Oh, what a pal was Mary,
  Oh, what a pal was she.
An angel was born on Easter morn
  And God sent her down to me.
Heart of my heart was Mary,
  Soul of my soul divine.
Though she is gone, love lingers on
  For Mary, old pal of mine.

I remember the tune too and, when prevailed under certain conditions, I can belt it out with suitable actions.

Probably the biggest music hall star in any Coliseum pantomime was Neil Kenyon, who seemed to me to be a cross between Harry Lauder and Will Fyffe. He packed the Coliseum, no mean feat, and I felt he was the thinking man's Scotch comic.

G.H. Elliot, the 'Chocolate Coloured Coon', was at his height then and was usually backed by Scotch comics who were Glasgow favourites. I remember especially Power and Bendon, whose famous act, 'Mendin' A Door', they managed to work into the pantomime too. Power played the foreman and Bendon was the apprentice. The lines most appreciated by the audience (who knew the whole thing off by heart) went:

BENDON   Well, Ah think —
POWER   You're no' peyed tae think. You're nothin'.
BENDON   An' whit are you?

POWER   Ah'm the gaffer.

BENDON   That's a great joab you've goat — gaffer ower nothin'!

That brought the house down among all those present who had gaffers.

I have mentioned that the Coliseum had the biggest stage in Glasgow. Once I saw a full-scale circus there, including all the traditional equestrian acts. In contrast, I also saw the famous Japanese film-star of silent days, Sessue Hayakawa (later to appear when talking pictures arrived) in a one-act play which concluded with the hero committing hara-kiri, fortunately with his back to the audience. The curtain came down to rapturous applause and rose again to show Mr Hayakawa smiling and bowing to the audience without a spot of blood on him.

Less fortunate was Mark Sheridan, an English comedian who had a Napoleon complex. He toured in revues and, if possible, he would make an appearance somewhere in the show as Napoleon, whom he strongly resembled. His last revue was at the Coliseum. I didn't see it but I gathered from reports that it was inadequately rehearsed and inefficiently presented. At any rate, it got the bird from the Glasgow audience. Next day it also got the bird from the Glasgow newspapers (there were seven of them then).

That afternoon Mark Sheridan took a tram-car to Kelvingrove Park, selected a secluded spot, and shot himself. He died in the Western Infirmary near by.

Another theatrical star who had serious trouble at the Coliseum was the Great Dr Walford Bodie. He claimed to be the highest paid stage performer in the world. Although this was never substantiated, Bodie did live in a castle at Macduff on the North-East coast of Scotland. The flag was always run up on the mast at Macduff when Bodie was in residence. The rest of the time he spent touring his electric magic show, *Fun Aboard an Ocean Liner*.

I was fortunate enough to meet the Great Dr Walford Bodie, when he took part in a BBC radio programme of mine. With his jet black hair and his twirling moustache he looked rather like the traditional stage conception of Mephistopheles. He spoke in a deep, impressive voice and had the manner of a Grand Seigneur.

I have already mentioned Frank and Doris Droy of the Queen's Theatre pantomime. They came into the Bodie saga. Frank ran an act called the De Roy Sisters and Frank. But he wasn't satisfied with working for other people and decided to have a concert party of his own. He got four other artists to join the party and engaged a hall at Macduff for a week. At the end of the week they had not collected enough money to pay for the hire of the hall, far less themselves. Fate, in the person of the Great Dr Walford Bodie, stepped in. Word came to him, in some way or other (remember, he had mystic powers) of the plight of the concert party. He not only paid for the hire of the Macduff hall but offered an engagement to the De Roy Sisters and Frank. They were glad to accept.

They had hardly agreed when Dr Bodie said he would give a demonstration of his powers. He was a hypnotist and started off by mesmerising Doris Droy. He could make her lift her arm at his command, but even the Great Bodie could not put Doris in a complete trance. With Doris's sister it was different. She went into a trance at once and the Great Bodie had complete control over her. He was very pleased at the result of his experiment and presented Doris's sister with an autographed photograph of himself. 'Do not be surprised,' he said, 'if I frequently visit you in your dreams.'

Doris's sister was terrified. That night, when she and Doris went back to their little room in Macduff, she said she couldn't sleep. She was certain that the spectral form of the Great Dr Walford Bodie was going to materialise at any moment. Doris and she got into bed and, to scare away spirits, left the oil lamp burning.

They did go to sleep, although they fought against it as long as they could, assisted by the elements outside, for it was a dark and stormy night. When they awoke in the morning they looked at each other and screamed. They had turned black. What new and awful wizardry was this? Then they realised that the oil lamp had gone out, and the soot had flown around the room. Much of it had settled on Doris and her sister.

Off went the De Roy Sisters and Frank with the Great Dr Walford Bodie and *Fun Aboard an Ocean Liner*. They travelled in a van which also held the elaborate equipment for the show plus the scenery. Each time they arrived at a hall they helped to put the scenery up. It was the penny geggie regime all over again.

Besides working with the scenery, they sold programmes and took tickets at the door. Doris not only provided the songs when necessary but also appeared as the nurse in the great electrical scene in which Dr Bodie 'cured' people of any ailment they happened to have. Her sister came on to be hypnotised and show that the Great Bodie had complete control over human beings. When he snapped his fingers and brought her back to normality she hadn't the slightest notion what she had been doing.

Fun Aboard an Ocean Liner had a break of two weeks and the De

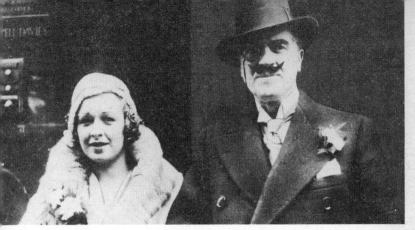

The Great Dr Walford Bodie, MD, on his wedding day, 1932.
(GLASGOW HERALD)

Roy Sisters and Frank returned to Glasgow. There Doris's sister made it clear that she was never going back to Bodie. In fact, she had decided to accept the proposal of a young man she knew and was going to get married as soon as possible. There was no alternative. Frank had to write to Macduff and announce that all was over between the De Roy Sisters and Frank and the Great Dr Walford Bodie. It was then that they formed their act of Frank and Doris Droy and eventually started their long season in the Queen's Theatre pantomimes.

The Great Bodie managed to survive this desertion. Indeed, he seemed to thrive. He was doing so well that he got a week's engagement at the Coliseum Theatre, Glasgow. He was billed as the Great Dr Walford Bodie, MD. Round the Coliseum entrance were hung crutches and all manner of medical aids to serious illness. These, it was announced, were the implements which had belonged to the vast number of people cured by Dr Bodie.

The medical students at Glasgow University took a poor view of this and their feelings were made plain in the Press. In interviews, when asked to reply, poured scorn on the students and asked what could you expect from people who cadged Carnegie grants?

This brought an immediate response. The following night most of the audience in the Coliseum were medical students. From the moment the curtain went up they expressed their displeasure with the Great Bodie. When other acts were on the stage they were perfectly quiet but the wizard had only to appear to be received, with shouts of 'Fake!' the least of the vituperation. The manager of the Coliseum decided to drop the fire curtain.

The sight of the curtain descending sent the students wild. From all parts of the theatre they attacked the stage and they were almost behind the fire curtain when the police arrived, summoned by the anxious manager. Several of the ringleaders were arrested. Among them was a young man named Osborne H. Mavor. This was, as far as I know, his first contact with the stage. It was by no means his last, for the time came when he gave up medicine and took to writing plays under the name of James Bridie.

The newspapers carried the story of the stramash at the Coliseum next morning and by the time the arrested students appeared in the police court public opinion was strongly on their side. It was reinforced when Dr Walford Bodie, MD, appeared as a witness and was asked what the letters 'MD' stood for. His reply was that MD stood for 'Merry Devil'.

The students were found guilty and were fined, as they say, a 'derisive' amount. All the fines were paid on the spot, and at the University O.H. Mavor and his friends were regarded as heroes.

Whether or not this was a contributing factor to the decision of the Coliseum to drop their stage shows and go into films I do not know. But I remember, in 1925, going to see Douglas Fairbanks in the silent version of *The Thief of Baghdad*. When I say silent, I mean that no sound came from the screen. There was plenty of sound from a big orchestra in the pit. We had had to join a long queue, but we felt it was worth it.

The time came, in January 1929, when the Coliseum showed the first talkie seen and heard in Glasgow. It was *The Jazz Singer*, starring Al Jolson. I recollect that Glasgow audiences thought the most remarkable bit about it was not the dialogue or the music, but the sound of bacon sizzling in a pan over a fire.

This may have been because various forms of talking picture had already been seen in Glasgow. They were usually 'shorts' and consisted of a performance by a singer. I recall the release of a full-length film in which some of the reels had sound applied and others were still silent. The effect, as you can imagine, was remarkable. So people were getting accustomed to voices coming from the screen, but *The Jazz Singer* was the first talkie with frying bacon!

It was not long before Glasgow cinemas changed to the talking pictures or, if they couldn't afford the new medium, closed down. The Coliseum became merely one of many and, when the slump in cinema-going came, it was one of the first to give up the ghost.

I'm sorry to see it empty and neglected. But I'll always remember it for Fred Barnes and the Great Dr Walford Bodie, MD.

THE
LONE
RANGER

I CALL THE PAVILION
Theatre in Renfield Street 'the Lone Ranger' because it is the only theatre in Scotland which exists entirely on what it takes at the door. It has no grants and no subsidies. For all I know, it may be the only theatre in Britain without a grant of some sort. This would not happen in Russia, where they regard the music hall as one of the arts, just as they do the circus. It's a great feather in the cap of successive managements that they have succeeded in keeping the Pavilion going.

The theatre opened on 29 February 1904, so that makes it 82 years of age. It is a comfortable place with only one fault — the bars are not big enough. (This is a personal problem. Perhaps some theatregoers are not interested.)

What it does have is a sliding roof, the only theatre in Scotland I know with such a device. I have been lucky enough to see the operation, but only once. Every now and then Glasgow has a heat wave in what we politely call our summer. I was at Tommy Morgan's summer show on one scorching night. It was the second house and the place was stifling. Just after the interval there was a rolling sound above us and we looked up to see the roof sliding majestically back. It was wonderful. The audience gave a great combined sigh of relief, then actually applauded the operation. The stars were shining bright and the only problem when the show restarted was whether to look at the stars in the sky or the stars on the stage. As far as I know, the sliding roof can still be operated, but I have heard no word of it being in use since that magic night.

And talking of stars, they all appeared there, including the inevitable one-act play performed by Sarah Bernhardt in her declining years. Charlie Chaplin is said to have appeared among the large cast in the Fred Karno knockabout troupe.

I was too young to have seen most of them but I especially wish I had been able to see Little Tich and Harry Fragson. At home we had gramophone records of both of them and I knew their songs off by heart. Little Tich was a tiny man who wore very long boots. Always in his act he'd do a dance which ended with him upright on his toes, still dancing. My own favourite Tich song was entitled 'I'm the Don of the Don Juans' and included the line, 'I have to carry a walking stick to keep the girls away.'

In England they have a habit of calling small men 'Tich'. I heard it often when I was in the Army during the Second World War, and I often wondered if the people who used the nickname realised that it had come from Little Tich himself.

Our records of Harry Fragson I also learned by heart. Fragson was French and I've sometimes thought that Maurice Chevalier copied him, consciously or unconsciously. He was best in somewhat dramatic songs and my favourite was 'Billy Brown of London Town', which told the story of an ordinary young Londoner joining up, going to war and being killed. I was a very sentimental boy (come to that, I'm now a very sentimental geriatric) and tears always came to my eyes when Harry Fragson reached his final verses.

The First World War was still going on and Fragson was now living in London. One day we were all shocked when the newspapers brought the news that he had been shot dead by his deranged father, whom he looked after.

Another star at the Pavilion was the London comedian, Arthur Roberts. He was the first person I had to interview for my London agent who specialised on 'signed articles'. The topic the agent chose for me was 'What's Wrong with the Music Hall Today?' A perennial topic, in my experience.

Arthur Roberts was appearing in a 'Veterans of Variety' show at the old Metropole in Stockwell Street and I arranged to call at his nearby theatrical digs. He must have forgotten this because, when I arrived and told his landlady of my appointment, she took me straight to the door, knocked and threw it open. There was the great comedian, almost naked, rubbing something that smelled like liniment on his lower back. He roared and I made my exit.

'Just wait,' said the landlady, who obviously knew her Arthur.

So I waited and it was not long ere the door opened and a fully dressed Roberts invited me in more or less affably. He explained that he suffered from arthritis 'or what I call Arthuritis'.

I got the impression that he wanted to tell me what was wrong with the music hall and was determined to lay waste the stage. That is what he did and I thought it advisable to tone down some of the more vituparate bits. Either he didn't remember them or else, on reflection, he agreed with me. Anyway, he signed the article and unknowingly set me on a new career.

Incidentally, the 'Veterans of Variety' were amazing. They sat on chairs in a half circle and, to be truthful, some of them looked barely alive, including Arthur Roberts. But, as soon as the compère announced him, he jumped up, strode to the footlights (they still had them then) and gave the audience an experience which I doubt any of them, including me, had ever had before. He was a wonderful music hall antique and, of all the Veterans, got the greatest applause. I doubt, though, if the article I 'ghosted' for him made any real impression on the music hall of that time, a time that is already in the distant past.

At the Pavilion I had the perfect pleasure of hearing Layton and Johnstone perform. Everyone knew of them, because they were so often on the wireless but seeing them putting over their very individual songs was something approaching ecstasy. In case any of my readers don't know, Turner Layton and Clarence Johnstone were a coloured couple and they sang with dark chocolate voices.

While they were appearing at the Pavilion, the idiosyncratic Seymour Hicks was in one of his farcical comedies at the Alhambra. I 'ghosted' for him as well, and was bidden to lunch with him at the Malmaison. He ordered a well-done steak. I don't know whether the chef didn't approve of well-done steaks (quite a lot of them don't), but this one was coal black. Seymour Hicks called Luigi, the head waiter, over. Waving his hand at the steak, Hicks said, 'I'm very fond of Layton and Johnstone, but I don't want to eat them.'

Talking of singers, the Pavilion was the first theatre in which I saw Donald Peers of 'By a Babbling Brook' fame. He had a good reception and was moved to thank the audience profusely. 'Especially,' he said, 'my good friend, Jock, sitting there in the audience.' His good friend Jock turned out to be the Hon. John Weir, son of Lord Weir. I knew he had an ambition to be the Scottish Noel Coward, because I wrote radio scripts with him. I always waited to see if Donald Peers would sing a number written by John, but the brook ceased to babble without one coming along.

The manager of the Pavilion in those days was a bucolic type named Jock Kirkpatrick. He was always putting people who called him 'Mr Kilpatrick' right. He was of the old school and turned out in top hat, white tie and tails. His great friend among newspaper people was Harold Dickson of the old Evening News and Harold had an arrangement with his editor that he would cover the Pavilion performance every Monday evening. Jock Kirkpatrick invariably invited Harold up to his private room for a small refreshment, which was sometimes so big that Harold would miss part of the show.

On one of these occasions Harold arrived at the News office early on Tuesday morning and handed the sub-editor who was responsible for the theatre notices his review of the previous evening's show at the Pavilion. The sub-editor was rather baffled at one point where Harold referred to one performer's success with his light railway. He took the copy through to Harold and asked him what this light railway business was. Harold said, 'Oh, it's absolutely marvellous. This chap has a wee railway which starts from the stage and goes up to the boxes, then round the front of the dress circle and back to the stage. Never seen anything like it.'

So the notice appeared and the Editor of the Evening News, in due course, read his first edition. He summoned Harold at once and asked him what the railway was.

Harold was frank. 'To tell you the truth,' he replied, 'I was talking to Jock Kirkpatrick at the time and I missed that act. But I know it's all right because I took it from the Glasgow Herald crit.'

So they looked up the appropriate page in the Herald and found that its critic had commended a comedian for his 'light raillery'.

I'm afraid to say that I wasn't as popular with Jock Kirkpatrick as Harold was. I had this strange habit of telling the truth, as I saw it. Once I was condemned to sit through a distinctly tatty 'French' revue, which was dirty, badly done and boring. I indicated this in my Citizen review and added that the only French you needed to know was the meaning of 'Double entendre'.

The first edition was hardly out ere Jock was on the 'phone. He was put on to the Assistant Editor and demanded, 'Who was that so-and-so Sunday school teacher you sent to our show last night?' This had one good effect. I was no longer condemned to the Pavilion — I got the Empress at St George's Cross instead!

Not that I mean to run down the Pavilion. I think I have said enough already to indicate how much I admire the place. And I'll always be grateful to the Pavilion for putting on Billy Connolly when he was good.

My first view of Mr Connolly was when he was one half of a double turn called the Humblebums. The other half was the very good musician, Gerry Rafferty. Billy did all the talking. 'We are the Humblebums,' he would say. 'I'm the humble one.' He also introduced the items.

When next seen, he was one of the organisers of *The Great Northern Welly Boot Show*, put on for a week in a Glasgow theatre. We met when we both appeared in a Scottish Television chat show, which Billy enlivened by playing a couple of numbers from the 'Welly Boot' operation. He was obviously an up-and-coming lad.

Then he got his big chance at the Pavilion and grabbed it with both hands. I still remember how entrancingly funny he was. He spent a good deal of the time recalling his school days and told a story about one of his lady teachers who was perched sideways on a tall stool while she tried to educate her pupils. She had forgotten to do up one side of her skirt and through the gap a bright red cloth was in view. Billy whispered to his pal, 'D'ye think that's her knickers?' 'Don't be daft,' replied the pal. 'That's a blanket!'

There was non-stop laughter from the Pavilion audience. I was looking around them, enjoying their enjoyment, when my eye lit on one of the elderly doorkeepers. He stood there and watched the Connolly performance with a grim expression. He'd probably thrown out people for saying less. He also looked as if he couldn't quite believe it.

Maybe that's what is wrong with me nowadays. I find Mr Connolly no longer funny, except in a macabre sort of way. Sometimes, on my visits to the People's Palace on Glasgow Green, I make a special point of going to see John Byrne's portrait of Billy. How I wish he was still like that.

I have mentioned that the Pavilion occasionally presented the drama — Sarah Bernhardt, for example. I recall other examples. One was perhaps an ill-conceived idea to put on a touring company in a very light comedy, *The Young Person in Pink*. The cast was headed by that excellent veteran comedienne, Sydney Farebrother. It was just the wrong thing for Pavilion audiences, especially on a Friday and Saturday.

I'm not sure what the punters expected, but this very English frothy stuff was not it. The audience interrupted with various suggestions of their own. Suddenly on the Friday night Miss Fare-brother stopped the play and delivered a few observations of her own on the manners of Glasgow audiences. This provoked her audience to near fury, so much so that the police were called. They were in attendance on the Saturday night as well but, apart from an undercurrent of disfavour, there were no more scenes.

Obviously, this was just a case of faulty booking. *The Young Person in Pink* might have done quite well at the King's or the Theatre Royal, in both of which Sydney Farebrother's name meant something.

Certainly the Pavilion audiences took the Scottish National Players to their bosom. Several times the Players put on one-act plays in a music-hall tour of Scotland and they were very popular indeed, as they should have been, given the calibre of their actors. An immensely popular full-length play at the Pavilion was *The Sash*, with Andrew Keir as an Orangeman wearing 'the sash my father wore'. He gave a brilliant performance as the man who couldn't stand the sight of green and hated the idea of his children calling him 'father'. He was surrounded by an excellent cast and the play itself, though rich comedy on the surface, had a lot of deep meaning in it.

The Sash did several seasons, every one of them successful, so much so that Keir decided to put on a series of plays at the Pavilion and ran a competition for playwrights. Out of the plays submitted he picked one called *The Bigot*, which was based on the same background as *The Sash*.

I went to the first night. An audience which obviously included a large number of 'Sash' devotees waiting in happy expectation. I don't know what went wrong. It was very difficult to discover whether there was any good in the play or not. The actors did not seem to know their lines and substituted a stream of well-worn Glasgow invective which became distressingly monotonous. I was not the only one who walked out of the theatre at the interval. *The Bigot* lasted only one week. It was a great pity, for Andrew Keir is a fine actor and, with the right plays, might have founded a new company in Scotland.

As I write, the Pavilion pantomime of *Cinderella* has just finished its run, with Andy Cameron and a host of well-known faces in the cast. It was put on in association with Radio Clyde and produced by Jimmy Logan. I felt it was an earnest of the future success for a theatre which deserves to succeed.

TEN

KING
OF THE
KING'S

I HAVE SEEN A NUMBER of great performances at the King's Theatre, but the one which I especially treasure is the first appearance in Glasgow as a leading man of Laurence Olivier. I read as much as I could of what happened in the London theatres and I had noticed the name of Olivier but knew little of him. Then it was decided that a play called *The Royal Family of Broadway* should be produced at the King's before going to London.

The Royal Family of Broadway dealt with the Barrymores — John, Ethel and Lionel. Brian Ahearne was coming across from America to play the part of John Barrymore. The London producers decided that they would have to change the title of the piece as it might be construed to be a slight on our own Royal Family. So they changed the title to *Theatre Royal*, which was rather confusing to Glasgow theatregoers who were somewhat bewildered that *Theatre Royal* was actually at the King's.

For filming reasons, Brian Ahearne was not able to appear in the try-out at the King's and it was announced that the young Laurence Olivier would take the part of John Barrymore in Glasgow. At the same time it was revealed that Brian Ahearne was going to fly across the Atlantic to be at the opening night at the King's.

Ahearne (whose death at the age of 83 has just been announced as I write these words) duly arrived. The setting was an enormous room in the Barrymore mansion, with a balcony high above the floor. Lionel Barrymore was there in his wheel chair. Ethel Barrymore was emoting powerfully. There was no sign of John. Suddenly a figure appeared on the balcony, jumped to the railing, launched himself off in a somersault, landed on his feet and immediately went into a speech. Laurence Olivier had arrived.

Brian Ahearne flew back to America next day and never appeared as John Barrymore in this country. Olivier went on from success to success. The next time I saw him in Glasgow was his brilliant performance in *The Entertainer*, when he shocked his elderly lady admirers no end. Perhaps they had never seen the spectacle of a fading Cockney comic trying desperately to keep his end up. I was lucky enough (if lucky is the right word) to have seen one or two, so I could appreciate everything that Olivier did.

Another remarkable first night at the King's was C.B. Cochran's production of the musical, *Ever Green*. As usual, Cochran did everything in tremendous style. He took a mansion house in the West End of Glasgow for a month and his wife joined him there while rehearsals were proceeding. The first revolving stage ever seen in Glasgow was fitted to the King's. An international cast arrived for a month's rehearsals. They were headed by Jessie Matthews and Sonnie Hale and included a famous French comedian in the style of Maurice Chevalier, plus a hardly-known Midlands comic called Albert Burdon, who had been picked for stardom by Cochran. There was also a variety of assorted animals.

At last the first night came. Glasgow was agog. We had seen some big shows but nothing as big as this, and certainly nothing had had so much trumpet blowing. The time came for the start of *Ever Green*, but nothing happened. We could hear hammering going on behind the curtain and there was a rumour that the revolving stage was refusing to revolve. At length C.B. Cochran appeared before the curtain and apologised to the audience. There were some technical difficulties, he said, but he hoped we would forgive him. He got a round of applause.

The curtain actually rose on the show just over an hour late. It was certainly a most elaborate production, perhaps over-elaborate. Jessie Matthews was superb and Sonnie Hale backed her well. All kinds of speciality acts performed. The animals went by two-by-two. The audience were wilting but they were determined to get their money's worth. The show ended just after midnight with C.B. Cochran taking a bow and assuring us that the various wee mistakes would be put right before *Ever Green* ended its several weeks' run in Glasgow.

Mind you, he kind of spoiled the effect a little by saying at a big

Glasgow lunch to which he'd been invited that he was always delighted to put on a new show in Manchester because the audiences were so good. Well, you can't be right all the time.

At the King's I saw John Gielgud's *Hamlet* and was so impressed that I wrote a glowing notice. Arthur Hedderwick, the Editor of the Evening Citizen, called me into his room and congratulated me. Then he added, 'But really, Mr House, you can't criticise a performance of *Hamlet* properly unless you saw Johnston Forbes-Robertson in the part.'

The King's was a fine theatre — it still is. It was there that I was introduced to the D'Oyly Carte Opera Company in Gilbert and Sullivan. I had an aunt who was a school teacher and every time I mentioned a show I'd seen, she would say, 'Ah, but have you ever seen *The Mikado*?' I was sixteen at the time and you know what you're like when you're sixteen. I took a complete scunner to *The Mikado*. I had never heard of the thing, but I knew I'd have no time for it if it appealed to elderly people like Aunt Annie. (She'd be in her late thirties at the time!)

I determined that wild horses wouldn't drag me to see *The Mikado*, but my Aunt Annie did. She arranged a party of four and announced that she would pay for the seats. We were to meet at the Early Doors of the Pit Stalls at the King's Theatre at 6 o'clock and queue for a performance that would not start until 7.30. That was the last straw, but what could I do? I didn't want to get into family trouble.

So we waited and waited and, when we got in and found pit stall seats behind the empty front stalls, we just kept on waiting. My Aunt Annie had brought chocolates to while away the hours. At last the rich folk arrived and took their seats in front of us. The orchestra tuned up, the auditorium lights went down and the curtain arose on the male chorus of the D'Oyly Carte company singing, 'We are gentlemen of Japan'.

At that very moment I was captured and have been daft about Gilbert and Sullivan ever since (though I must admit that I prefer Gilbert to Sullivan). Of course, the D'Oyly Carte company of those days was a bright and shining one. Henry Lytton was in his prime and his Ko-Ko was only equalled by the enormous yet light-footed Leo Sheffield as Pooh-Bah. Bertha Lewis was a magnificent Katisha and Darrell Fancourt a terrifying Mikado. Why had I been missing this for so long? I decided that elderly people might be worth paying some attention to.

Oddly enough, *The Mikado* was the only Gilbert and Sullivan opera that my Aunt Annie had ever seen. Maybe she was afraid to go to any of the others in case they were not up to its standard. But I was so entranced that I went to one Gilbert and Sullivan piece after another, as long as I had the money. (You couldn't do much on a CA apprentice's salary.)

It took me some years to go right through the D'Oyly Carte repertoire and I was delighted when they revived two shows which had been dropped — *Ruddigore* (which Queen Victoria didn't like because of the title), and *The Sorcerer,* in which Henry Lytton sang, 'My name is John Wellington Wells. I'm a dealer in magic and spells', and made audiences wonder why this delightful charade had been lost for so long. I made up the rest of the Gilbert and Sullivan canon by seeing some pieces which the D'Oyly Carte never put on — for example, *Utopia Limited,* which had the British Cabinet sitting in a half-circle in minstrel style and discussing affairs of state in the same manner. I should think it would be very popular if brought back today. These forgotten Gilbert and Sullivan tit-bits were revived by Glasgow amateur operatic companies.

The King's was sometimes the only theatre in Glasgow which did not present a pantomime at Christmas time. They went in for big scale musical shows and so I saw *The Student Prince, The Vagabond King, The Desert Song, Lilac Time* and *Rose Marie.* One night I was in the wings when the show was *Rose Marie.* There was a 'flu epidemic in Glasgow at the time. The big number, the show-stopper, was 'Totem Tom-Tom', in which a long line of male dancers, acrobats and chorus girls went through the most energetic dance routine I have ever seen. As girls came off the stage to circle round and appear again on the other side, they were dropping unconscious. A group of stage hands and other helpers were lifting them and carrying them off to receive attention. 'Totem Tom-Tom' ended with not much more than half the dancers it started with.

Ivor Novello appeared in various of his confections, although sometimes his part was taken by a permanent understudy who was so like the boss that you could hardly tell the difference. Richard Tauber enchanted the audience by singing 'You are my heart's delight' in *The Land of Smiles.* He had most of his meals in Geneen's Kosher Hotel in the Gorbals, wise man that he was. Mrs Geneen was a wonderful woman and her food was wonderful too.

The King's had only one problem — summer time. For a while, each summer, they ran a series of well-worn comedies, presented by the same touring companies every year. I recall, in particular, When Knights Were Bold, The Private Secretary and *Are You A*

Mason? They were not bad at all but they ran out of audiences. More and more often the King's (in common with some other Glasgow theatres) was 'closed for refit', as the euphemism went.

In 1933 the management had an idea. All up and down the Clyde coast the local summer shows were doing wonderful business. Why not put on a summer show on a bigger scale in Glasgow? So *Half-Past Eight* was born, so timed that it gave Glaswegians the chance to enjoy the good weather (which we seemed to have then) and end the evening at the theatre. They engaged Jack Edge as the comedian and put a good company around him. The show became popular and the King's felt they had the answer to the summer at last.

The following summer they starred Billy Caryll and Hilda Mundy and the cast included the Tiller Girls and a well-worn couple of comedians, Wheeler and Wilson. Caryll and Mundy were an instant success. Billy was a very sharp comedian with one of the best drunk acts I've seen. His wife was more than just a foil. Hilda was a critic as well and gave as good as she got. With the previous year's experience, the management had put more money into the show and it was regarded as every bit as good as many of the revues seen in the rest of the year. I remember an elderly lawyer friend of mine who said to me, 'Saw that chap everybody's talking about — Billy Carlisle — at the King's last night. Very good but — eh, isn't he a wee bit near the bone?'

Caryll and Mundy returned to *Half-Past Eight* the following year and received an ovation when they made their first appearance on the opening night. The summer show was established and it ran for years with such welcome visitors as Beryl Reid, Jimmy Jewel and Ben Warriss, and then, at last, a Scotch comic — Dave Willis. *Half-Past Eight* went to Edinburgh and paved the way for the much bigger international show, *Five Past Eight*, at the Alhambra.

It's odd to think that this noble theatre, the King's, is now, officially, a 'public hall' belonging to Glasgow District Council. Nevertheless, it is the leading theatre in the city. I do not include the Theatre Royal in that category because it is, properly, now an Opera House, although it is used for plays and pop groups when neither Scottish Opera nor the Scottish Ballet are performing.

As far as the King's is concerned, the days of the big musical shows are over and the winter and spring are given over to pantomime, in which Stanley Baxter, Rikki Fulton and Johnnie Beattie alternate as the stars.

Billy Caryll and Hilda Mundy in *Half-Past Eight*
at the King's, 1935. (GLASGOW HERALD)

Lupino Lane and Teddie St Denis on their way to fame in
the 'prior to London' opening at the Alhambra of *Me and My Girl*.
(GLASGOW HERALD)

ELEVEN

THE FAVOURITE'S DOWN!

I HAVE ALWAYS BEEN attracted to the theatres of Glasgow, but there was one which I really loved. It was the Alhambra, just a step along Waterloo Street from three of my favourite eating places, the Malmaison, the Grosvenor and the One-O-One. We always dined, before or after the show, in one of them, even if I had to write my review for early next morning. The opulent air in the Alhambra appealed to my hedonistic tendencies.

There was the smell of lingering cigar smoke, for example. I have never smoked in my life but I bask in the scent of cigars. Although it was a big theatre it somehow had a cosiness about it. I've always been sorry that I wasn't at its opening night in 1910 but I was only four years old at the time, and my father and mother must have thought I was a bit young for the occasion. However, I made up for that later because I saw my first pantomime there in 1916 and, while the Alhambra existed, I was probably there more often than in any other Glasgow theatre.

I never missed an Alhambra pantomime, even when I was in the Army. Somehow or other I wangled leave every New Year, mainly because I was one of the few Scots in the outfit still living in Scotland. The thing to do was to volunteer to act as the Orderly Officer over the Christmas break and the grateful Sassenachs responded with a couple of extra days on the normal leave.

Already I have mentioned the fine pantomimes I saw at the Alhambra, particularly the Scottish ones. But if you ask me which stays most clearly in my memory, I must admit that it was *The*

Queen of Hearts, which had no Scots at all in the leading roles. The stars were Lupino Lane, Mona Vivian and A.W. Bascomb.

Bascomb, a wonderfully lugubrious comedian, played the Queen. Lupino Lane was the Knave of Hearts. Mona Vivian was the principal boy. I had lost my heart to her the first time I saw her in a touring revue at the Alhambra. She was small but bursting with vitality. Bascomb was a discovery for Glasgow. We had heard of his success in London but we couldn't imagine anyone who could make utter pessimism so funny.

Lupino Lane, of course, we knew well. All the Lupino family appeared in Glasgow theatres at various times. Stanley Lupino was famous for his musical shows. Barry Lupino did a solo act in the top music halls. In my opinion he was the funniest Lupino of the lot and I was always surprised that he was overshadowed by Stanley and Lupino Lane. The latter, of course, was multi-talented and was an acrobat, a dancer, a juggler and a comedian as well. It was difficult to place him in any class, but it could be said that, while he was funny, he wasn't as miraculously so as the other members of the clan.

His big scene in *The Queen of Hearts* was a trap-door act which occupied the whole of the proscenium. It was like the front of a block of flats with doors on various levels. Lane performed the most amazing acrobatics with a team of four French trap-door specialists. Its *raison-d'être* in the pantomime was that the Knave was being pursued by secret police who were trying to trap him so that he could be brought to justice for all his misdeeds.

The way the five of them hurled themselves in and out of the myriad doors baffles description. Lane was always eluding his pursuers by a hairsbreadth, and you never knew on which level he would next appear. The timing was perfection and, of course, Lane escaped and the chase ended. Even in the Moscow State Circus I have never seen anything like it.

Lupino Lane invited his father, Harry Lupino, to come up from London to see the show. The old man sat through the performance and then his son took him to supper. All this time he never said a word about the trap-door scene, though he praised the pantomime. At last, in desperation, his son asked him what he thought about the acrobatics. Old Harry Lupino shook his head sadly. 'There was a wrinkle in your tights,' he said.

I saw *The Queen of Hearts* on the first night, half-way through the season and on its last night. In true pantomime tradition Lupino Lane turned it upside down. He excelled himself in the trap-door scene. Just as it was rushing to its climax, he presented each of the

French performers, in turn and with perfect timing, with a bottle of whisky as a farewell present.

And then, near the end of the show, the Knave of Hearts fought a duel with the principal boy and the scene climaxed when Mona Vivian won, the Knave fell and she put one foot on his chest and waved her sword triumphantly to the audience. Not on the last night, though. They started fencing and the Knave simply refused to be beaten. Eventually Mona Vivian's sword went spinning through the air, she fell and the Knave put his foot on her chest and waved to the now hysterical audience.

Perhaps the most surprising show which came to the Alhambra was Lupino Lane's *Me and My Girl*. It was in October 1937, with the great Empire Exhibition due to open in Glasgow the following Spring. Lupino Lane was always popular in Glasgow and I went to the opening night with high expectations.

Just in case you don't know, *Me and My Girl* tells the story of a Cockney lad who suddenly becomes a Baronet because of the death of some far-out relation. He arranges a party where his friends from Lambeth will meet the aristocratic relations he didn't know existed. The production, of course, was 'prior to London'. It must be admitted that the show seemed dire. Lupino Lane hardly raised a laugh.

Just as we were approaching the interval, when I could go and drown my sorrows and wonder what on earth I was going to say about this obvious flop, Lupino Lane invited his High Society guests to join him and his Cockney mates in 'The Lambeth Walk'.

It was a riot. The subdued audience suddenly brightened up. By the time 'The Lambeth Walk' ended the first act, *Me and My Girl* had turned from flop to success. When we went to the Circle Bar for, as the best people say, a wee refreshment, the audience was bubbling over. The second act was an enormous improvement on the first and the evening ended with an ovation for the cast.

At this time I was doing a weekly BBC radio programme to which I brought various guests — usually celebrities or notorieties who were in Glasgow. I invited Lupino Lane, his leading lady, who called herself Teddie St Denis although she was really a Glasgow girl playing a Cockney, the composer of *Me and My Girl*, Noel Gay.

They were delighted to be asked, came to the studio, were interviewed and Lupino Lane and Teddie St Denis sang the two big hits of the show, 'Me and My Girl' and 'The Lambeth Walk'. And they did this free, not even suggesting a fee. I can't imagine that happening now.

But it could be said to have paid enormous dividends. *Me and My Girl* went on to London, where it ran for over fifteen hundred performances: and 'The Lambeth Walk' actually became the theme song of the Empire Exhibition. When the bands played it and it was relayed all over Bellahouston by the loud speakers, everyone joined in, especially with the ecstatic shout of 'Oi!' Every night, even when it was pouring, as it often did that Summer, crowds would promenade the whole gigantic park, singing 'The Lambeth Walk'.

The Exhibition was a favourite visiting place for the then Queen Mother, the redoubtable Queen Mary. She visited it every time she was in Scotland and even made a special trip on the closing night when, in spite of the worst downpour of the season, it was packed with people, all singing 'The Lambeth Walk'. It is not known, however, whether Her Majesty joined in the shout of 'Oi!'

Jack Buchanan, as I have already mentioned, made many appearances in his favourite Glasgow. His musical comedies were, with one exception, fast, sweet-moving performances, for they had already been honed to perfection. The one exception was when he decided to present a first performance of a new musical, *Mr Whittington*. This was based loosely on the pantomime of Dick Whittington in rather the same genre as the Bobby Howes success, *Mr Cinders*, was based on the Cinderella pantomime.

As usual, Buchanan had done the production himself and it became obvious that, while most of the cast were well rehearsed, he was notably not. At one point he started a song and lost his words. He tried again and then said to the audience, 'I'd better dance.' So he danced to the rest of the music of the song. For once a Jack Buchanan musical was a disappointment in Glasgow, and the newspapers made that clear next day. The great man's only reply was to shake his head sadly and say, 'Glasgow doesn't understand first nights.'

Of the other Alhambra shows I recall with gratitude the many visits of 'The Co-Optimists', with Stanley Holloway, Davy Burnaby, Gilbert Childs (an enormously funny man), Phyllis Monkman, Laddie Cliff and Melville Gideon; Nikita Balieff with his 'Chauve Souris' and his fractured English; the 'Blackbirds' revue, with the almost unbelievable dancing of the Nicholas Brothers; and the long run of *My Fair Lady* when people came from all over Scotland to see the show because it was running only at the Glasgow Alhambra.

There was straight drama at the Alhambra too. The one which remains inderadicably lined on the tablets of my mind though a yesterday has faded from its page (not my words, W.S. Gilbert's), was the only appearance in Glasgow of the great film star, Pola Negri, and that's for personal reasons.

There was much excitement when it was announced that Pola Negri was coming to Glasgow in a one-act play. I had my own particular excitement when the Editor of the Evening Citizen called me into his office. 'Mr House,' he said, with what I thought was a twinkle in his eye, 'I have an interesting job for you.' He paused for effect. 'I want you to take Miss Pola Negri to lunch.'

To say that I was taken aback was an understatement. At that time I'd been in the Malmaison on several occasions and I realised that it must be the place to take an international film star. I was wondering if my good suit would be good enough, because I didn't think I had enough money to get a new one.

The problem did not arise. I mentioned to my superior, Colin Milne, that the Editor had given me the commission to take Pola Negri to lunch. Colin looked rather shame-faced. 'I'd better tell you what you've to do, Jack,' he said. 'The whole thing has been arranged with Pola Negri's publicity man. You've to meet her in her suite at the Central Hotel at 12 o'clock on Tuesday. There'll be a piper waiting there and the idea is that he'll pipe you and Pola Negri to Lang's in Royal Exchange Square and you'll give her lunch there.'

To say that I was appalled does not do justice to the situation. First of all, I did not want to be piped through the centre of Glasgow with Pola Negri. I'd made an exhibition of myself in aid of the Citizen on several occasions, but I felt this was carrying a daft story too far.

Second, Lang's was not the place for a lady. The clientele consisted almost entirely of Glasgow business men. They went there to have a quick lunch (or so it was said) of sandwiches and beer, though there was also hot soup in the winter months. To show that they were in a hurry to get back to business they did not take off their bowler hats. They helped themselves to whatever they required and pulled their own pints. Then they went to the cashier's desk and told her what they owed her. The cashier never questioned the stated sum.

But short changing the cashier was regarded as just as scoundrelly as cheating the Bank of Scotland and some of the business men had eagle eyes for misdoers. If they saw this happening they moved in at once, and a day or two later you'd see a small advertisement in the Personal Column of the Glasgow Herald that some visitor to Lang's had made a donation to charity in lieu of his peculation. Lang's was the first restaurant in the world to put its clientele on their honour and was mentioned in newspapers as far afield as New York and Hong Kong. It even got into Punch.

I tell you these things because I want to demonstrate the magnitude of the task with which I had been saddled. I could only hope that Pola Negri had a sense of humour.

I thought it would be a good idea to go to see her opening night at the Alhambra on the Monday before next day's lunch. This I did, and suffered more than ever. The one-act play was a two-hander and the other member of the cast was an English actor I had much admired. His name was Reginald Tate. Mercifully, I have forgotten the play but I think Miss Negri played the part of a spy, a sort of Mata Hari character. Mr Tate did his best, but could not rescue Miss Negri, who reminded me of the words of the notable Hollywood director, Billy Wilder, who, when he was ready for the actors to come on the set, would shout to his assistant, 'Right — bring on the face-makers.'

Let me confess that, thinking of the morrow, I had a bad night. But I felt even worse in the morning when I read the Glasgow newspapers. Each critic made no bones about the fact that he considered Pola Negri a bad actress in a bad play. Some commiserated with Reginald Tate. Can you imagine my feelings as I presented myself at the Central Hotel and sent word to Miss Negri's suite that I had arrived? I didn't see a piper anywhere but I assumed that he was tuning up somewhere outside.

I was given the number of the suite and went upstairs and knocked. The door opened and a worried-looking young woman confronted me. I explained that I had an appointment and she asked me to wait while she took in Miss Negri's breakfast. There was a bottle of whisky, a flagon of water and the morning newspapers on a tray. Each paper had been opened at the review of the previous night's performance, marked with a blue pencil.

My feeling was one of relief, because I realised that, if this was just breakfast going in, there was little chance of my taking Pola Negri to Lang's that day. Then I heard the most terrible swearing and the tearing of paper. I couldn't make out the words because they were in Polish but their meaning was abundantly clear.

After a while the worried-looking young woman came out of the bedroom and back to where I waited in the sitting room. She was shaking slightly. 'I don't think you should see Miss Negri this morning,' she said. 'How was this appointment arranged?' I told her about the publicity man's brilliant idea of a piping lunch at Lang's. 'Oh,' she said. 'he was sacked nearly two weeks ago.'

I went back to the Citizen office and reported to the Editor and Colin Milne. They couldn't stop laughing. As for me, I thought I might as well go to Lang's anyway. So I did, but did not pour myself a pint of beer. I stuck to large whiskies.

This was not my only confrontation with a film star. One of the last shows at the Alhambra was the appearance of Betty Grable in a musical called *The Pieceful Palace*. This strange name owed its origin to a tavern in a Wild West town where the proprietor couldn't spell. He meant 'Peaceful', of course. And the witty point the production made was that it wasn't peaceful at all. The Alhambra was to see its first production, on its way to London. There was some excitement in Glasgow that the great star with the lovely legs was to be among us. The whole week was booked out almost immediately. I was at the first night as critic of the Evening Times.

It was a lavish, big scale show with an enormous chorus. Apart from Betty Grable, the cast was more or less unknown, though obviously American. They included what was new in those days, a 'gay' cowboy. He worked hard but scarcely got a single laugh. Everybody in the show worked hard, too, with the exception of Betty Grable.

She made a wonderful appearance at the top of a huge stairway and was given an ovation as she descended the steps with a full view of the highly insured legs. What dialogue she had was uttered in a condescending tone as if she was the Queen of Hollywood talking to the peasants.

What bothered me was that Betty would start a song and render a couple of verses and chorus and then the chorus itself would close in around her and, lo and behold, you couldn't behold her. She just seemed to vanish. This went on all night and Grable was severely rationed. Well, the audience had seen Betty Grable, more or less, and there was another ovation at the final curtain. As we left the Alhambra an elderly friend of mine said with tears in his eyes, 'They don't make them like that any more.' He might have been quoting from the dialogue in *The Pieceful Palace*.

I felt the truth must be told, so I told it in the next day's Evening Times. My Editor, S.L. McKinlay, made quite a big spread of it. I mentioned the various things which were wrong with the show,

Molly Urquhart and Stanley Baxter in *Five Past Eight*.
(SCOTTISH THEATRE ARCHIVES)

including the sudden disappearances of the star, and concluded by
saying that it would surprise me if it lasted more than two weeks in
London.

I have to admit I was wrong. It lasted ten nights, even though
they had changed the name from *The Pieceful Palace* to something
more understandable. I do not write this to prove anything except
that I believe newspaper critics should always tell the truth as they
see it.

The end of the Alhambra came, strangely enough, with one of
its most popular shows. The old idea of *Half-Past Eight* had been

changed to *Five Past Eight* and, from a pleasant little summer revue, it was transformed into one of the most spectacular shows ever seen in Glasgow. Dick Hurran was in charge and he had big ideas. He engaged the topmost stars and surrounded them with, for example, the Bluebell Girls. Nothing was too magnificent for the Alhambra summer show.

Indeed, I recollect being in Paris and going to the Lido on the Champs Elysées. At least half of the Lido programme was composed of acts which I had already seen in *Five Past Eight* at the Alhambra. They were, perhaps, not quite so well presented because the Lido had a comparatively small stage. *Five Past Eight* at the Alhambra brought entrepreneurs from all over the world to see the show. Nothing in London came up to the standard set in Glasgow.

Scottish performers were occasionally used. One summer the star was Dickie Henderson and on the stage he encountered a beautiful young woman who turned out to be an expert on the Glasgow patter. She was Una McLean and, though she was well known as a local star, the *Five Past Eight* appearance really made her name. Stanley Baxter and Jimmy Logan were brought in, but it seemed that Dick Hurran regarded Scots as no more than quite good substitutes for top stars.

The climax of *Five Past Eight* came when the producer booked the new stars, Morecambe and Wise, for the show. Shortly before the opening night Morecambe had the first of his heart attacks. The contract had to be cancelled and, at very short notice, Dick Hurran had to find someone else. The only other comedian available was Norman Wisdom, and the story I heard was that his agent insisted that he would be paid more than Morecambe and Wise. For the first time *Five Past Eight* was a flop. It seemed to have priced itself out of the market.

Naturally, I don't blame Norman Wisdom in the least for this. It was about the time when the agents for top international acts were demanding more and more for their clients. The fact is, though, that the Alhambra lost so much money over the last *Five Past Eight* show that it never recovered and the only solution the proprietors had was to sell the building. And so Glasgow's favourite theatre was pulled down and replaced by one of these office blocks which, I dare say, have an importance of their own but mean nothing to me.

TWELVE

THE
ROYAL
ROAD

I CAN BOAST THAT I have made many stage appearances in the Theatre Royal. This is mainly owing to the fact that, when Scottish Television took the Royal over as its studios very few changes were made in the auditorium or on the stage. This saved STV a lot of money in the early days but it had a wonderful bonus for Scottish Opera. The television people built their new studios next door to the old theatre and Scottish Opera were able to move in to what was essentially the original place with the auditorium, the proscenium and the staging facilities virtually intact.

At the start of STV, I was one of the blue-eyed boys to the Canadian programme producer and to the various directors. I'd had a fair amount of experience with the BBC, especially on the Round Britain Quiz, so I was engaged as one of a team of four for an odd programme *I'll Buy That* (imported from Canada, of course).

The idea was that viewers brought along some unusual object for auction. Each sat in view of the audience (and, of course, the TV watchers) with their object also in view. The team sat on the other side of a curtain and had to try to guess what the object was. Each of us got four guesses and each time we got it wrong the contestant won £1 (which was worth a lot more than it is now). If we failed, the contestant would finish up with £16. We were not told, in so many words, that the show would be much funnier if we failed, but it was strongly hinted.

Indeed, there was one evening when I became absolutely convinced that the article was a penny-farthing bicycle. I can only assume that this was thought-transference or something else supernatural, for there was no hint in the first eight questions and answers that it was such a thing. I was the third questioner in the team and I asked questions that made me more and more certain that I was right. So, after my fourth question, I said 'A penny-farthing bicycle.' I was right!

When the programme was over my Canadian friend took me aside. More in sorrow than in anger he said, 'Jack, do you realise that chap brought the penny-farthing all the way from Falkirk, and now he's going back with only £12.'

I'll Buy That had a long run but I was glad when it ended. By this time, when I was going about my business in Glasgow, small boys would follow me shouting 'I'll buy that!' John Betjeman once asked me to take him through the Gorbals and everywhere we went the chorus followed us. I had to explain to him about the programme and he thought the whole thing was very funny. But most things in Glasgow appealed to his sense of humour. When we went back across the Clyde I showed him Glasgow University standing on top of Gilmorehill and said that a lot of people in the city considered it 'wedding cake architecture', he said, 'Oh, I don't know — I think it's rather fun.'

Among other things at Scottish Television, I appeared in the first studio pantomime. It was *Cinderella*, as conceived by Eddie Boyd. A number of STV 'regulars' were cast in the show. Larry Marshall was Buttons. Edith MacArthur played Prince Charming. Michael O'Halloran, the first announcer and a good actor, and I were the Ugly Sisters. We were given wigs and told that no make-up was necessary!

In the ballroom scene I had to dance with Edith MacArthur, which was very difficult because as Prince Charming she had to be the male partner while I, as an Ugly Sister, had to be the female. When, for some reason, I had to fall to the floor, I remembered Nellie Wallace in a Theatre Royal pantomime doing the same and shouting, to loud applause, 'The favourite's down!' So I did the same, just for old time's sake. No applause.

I had already appeared on the Royal stage before television was thought of (except, maybe, by John Logie Baird). Just as the King's had its succession of well-known farces during the summer, the Theatre Royal had a regular visiting company. But it was very far removed from farce. The Macdona Players made their annual visit in a Shaw repertoire and managed to attract audiences for a month or more.

Shaw had nearly as many devotees in Glasgow as had Gilbert and Sullivan. And, just as I saw all the Gilbert and Sullivan operas, so I saw all the Shaw plays. The Macdona company was led by a very individual actor named Esme Percy, and for years I couldn't imagine any other actor in the leading roles. The company was a good one and the standard was high.

Every now and then (though not as an annual occasion) Esme Percy would put on the full-length version of *Man and Superman*, including the Don Juan in Hell episode. The play lasts five-and-a-half hours, so the Royal opened its doors at 5.30 p.m. and had a 45-minutes interval so that the audience could get something so eat and drink before returning to the fray. As you can imagine, they had to be as devoted as the actors.

In the full show, there is a scene with a road below a high mountainside. Waiting for any passing car which can be held up and robbed is a group of brigands. They have a typically Shavian discussion of their respective beliefs while they wait.

It is obvious that the Macdona Players, as a touring company, could not carry enough actors to fill all the parts of the brigands. So they recruited amateurs in the various centres where they appeared. That was how I was engaged to take the part of the French Anarchist in *Man and Superman*.

The Scottish National Players had just been doing Barrie's *What Every Woman Knows* and had recruited a large number of amateurs for the election scene. Since I had brought along more recruits that anybody else (the entire male section of my amateur drama club) I was given the job of the leader of the mob. I can only imagine that I was on some sort of list of people available and that was how I got the invitation to join the cast of *Man and Superman*.

I knew most of the other amateurs who had been asked to the Theatre Royal. They included J.D.G. Macrae, who later became much better known as Duncan Macrae, and W.H.D. Joss, who has since made many appearances on television and radio. John Macrae was cast as a Cockney agitator with a fine line in street-corner elocution. Willie Joss, dressed in a rug and very little else, was the brigands' look-out on top of the mountain. He cut short our dialogue down below by suddenly running down the mountainside pointing O.P. and shouting 'Automobile! Automobile!'

We then gave up words for action and held up the car which drove on stage. It contained Shaw's hero, John Tanner, and his companions. That was the curtain and the start of the long interval. As far as the brigands were concerned, we went to our communal dressing room where we received our fee — ham sandwiches and beer.

When the recess was over and the audience had returned, the curtain went up on Hell. It consisted of rocks, with one clear space where Esme Percy, transformed from John Tanner into Don Juan, stood in a spotlight. Draped over the nearest rocks were three of his companions, now in the parts of Leonora, the Governor and the Devil. The play consisted of immensely long speeches by Don Juan, interrupted at appropriate moments by the others.

Since I was daft on acting, I didn't stay with the rest of the boys in our dressing room, even though there was more beer on tap. I went back down to the stage and stood in the wings during the Hell scene to see what happened. Since there were no exits and entrances during the scene, nobody worried about me. From where I was I viewed both upstairs and downstairs.

Under the rocks I could see that, with the exception of Esme Percy, each of the characters had his or her own prompter. Each prompter had a light above him and the script of the Hell scene in his hand. Occasionally (but not very often) Esme Percy would miss something out or put a speech in the wrong place, which was not surprising, given the enormous speeches involved. Then I could see the prompters riffling the script pages madly in order to find out where Don Juan had reached.

I felt the prompters were earning their money. One of them was Charles Macdona himself. The others were members of the company. I had never read the Don Juan in Hell scene (well, I'd started it but had to give up) so I had no idea what was missing nor, I am sure, had the audience. The important thing was that the scene kept flowing and the three players above the prompters seemed to come in right on cue.

After the last performance of *Man and Superman* the stage manager told me that I had been the best French Anarchist they had ever had. I bet he said that to all the French Anarchists. Although I knew it couldn't possibly be true, I felt no end chuffed, as we Thespians say.

The Theatre Royal specialised in good repertory companies. One of the finest was the Masque Players, who had a very high standard indeed. Once I saw them put on *The Cherry Orchard*. By a strange coincidence, a company of émigré Russian actors were putting on *The Cherry Orchard* in the old Lyric Theatre at the corner of Sauchiehall Street and Renfield Street at the same time. I thought it would be interesting to see the opening act by the

Masque Players at the Royal and then go down to the Lyric to see the Russian version of the rest of the play. It was remarkable to find that the Masque had treated *The Cherry Orchard* as tragedy, whereas the Russians, even though the language was incomprehensible to me, obviously played it as high comedy.

Many years later, on my first visit to Russia, I saw the Moscow Art Theatre present *The Cherry Orchard* and found that they played it as high comedy too. Can it be that we are more introspective than the Russians?

In August 1939, the Theatre Royal announced that they would be starting the season with a new group, the H.M. Tennent Repertory Company. The names of the players caused a sensation in Glasgow. I wish I could remember them and I actually met them at a cocktail party held in the Circle Bar of the Royal. But their opening play was not even chosen when Hitler started his attempt to conquer Europe. They went back to London and we will never know what we could have missed.

In fact, the way things turned out, we did not miss much. The Wilson Barrett Company arrived in Glasgow and started a season which spread to Edinburgh and Aberdeen. When they opened at the Theatre Royal they were run by Wilson Barrett and Jevan Brandon-Thomas, son of the Brandon-Thomas of *Charley's Aunt* fame. Their standard was high and they recruited several Scots, among whom was Simon Lack (original name, McAlpine) and James McKechnie.

With three theatres at their disposal they were able to make a six weeks' run of each play they produced, which was beneficial for a repertory group which can be rehearsing next week's show while this week's is still running. Eventually Jevan Brandon-Thomas retired and Wilson Barrett ran the company on his own.

I saw my first opera at the Theatre Royal. It was Gounod's *Faust* and I was immediately entranced. Mind you, it did not replace Gilbert and Sullivan in my affections, but I could see it was different! The two things which I still remember about *Faust* were 'The Soldiers' Chorus' and the performance of Kingsley Lark as Mephistopheles. I have always been specially attracted to the Devil and that's one reason I enjoyed some of Bridie's plays so much.

The company, of course, was Carl Rosa. They were another of our regular visitors and their annual visit to the Royal was a big event. Though Carl Rosa were a touring company they put on big productions. *The Flying Dutchman* was one of them and *The Mastersingers of Nuremberg* another.

Then there was an annual visit from an ad-hoc Italian Operatic Company. The Italian community in Glasgow supported this in a big way. Indeed, it could be said that there was as much enjoyment to be got out of the audience as the performance. Not for them the respectful attitude of opera-goers who are shocked if anyone applauds precipitately. Before a tenor's final top note, they were already clapping and shouting. They even demanded encores before the opera was allowed to proceed.

I was interested to note that one of their singers was not Italian, but Polish. She called herself Kyra Vayne and I first saw her when she appeared in a Metropole pantomime, *Bonnie Prince Charlie*, early in the war days. She had succeeded in escaping from Poland before the country was overrun by the Nazis and had arrived in Glasgow because it was a Polish centre. Miss Vayne played the principal boy and had probably the finest voice ever heard in the Metropole.

In those days the Glasgow Art Club gave temporary honorary membership to any operatic companies visiting the city, and in this case the principals of the show at the Theatre Royal were invited to supper at the Club. Lashings of pasta were laid on and suitable wine, though it was noticed that the male singers gave up their national drink in favour of ours.

Well, if the Italians were exuberant on the stage, it was nothing to how they behaved as the night went on. The moment they finished eating they started singing. And the more they drank the better they sang. The soirée went on, as far as anyone remembers, until four o'clock in the morning.

The Italians don't have a reputation for being tough, but I can't imagine anyone tougher than these opera singers, for they put on their usual ebullient performance that night in the Theatre Royal.

And so that brings me in musical stages to the present day of Scottish Opera. When they took over the Theatre Royal and transformed it into the magnificence it is now, I thought the millenium had arrived. Unfortunately my deafness gradually arrived as well. At first it didn't worry me overmuch. But one night, I sat in the First Circle and saw Sir Alexander Gibson raise his baton and start conducting. I could not hear a note. It was, of course, a pianissimo opening but I felt that was the end for me.

That doesn't stop me being proud of Glasgow's opera house and I can always recollect in tranquillity the beautiful sounds I have heard and the beautiful sights I have seen there.

THIRTEEN

END
OF
AN EMPIRE

THE   EMPIRE   WAS
undoubtedly the best-known Glasgow theatre in London. This
was because so many Southern comedians spread the myth that
the most dangerous thing you could do in the music hall business
was to appear at the Empire. One even described how he fainted
on the stage at the reception he got at the first house on Monday.
The dangers of the Empire were even chronicled in books by
authors who should have known better.

I'm not suggesting that Empire audiences were angels. They
could cut up rough if they didn't like the show on a Friday or a
Saturday night, when you might find characters who had been on
a pub crawl before they arrived at the second house. In all my visits
to the Empire I never once saw an act get the bird. I did, once or
twice, see players get a rather cold reception. But, as I have already
chronicled, I saw much worse at the Pavilion and no English
comedian has ever said a word against it.

There was sometimes soundless criticism at the Empire. I recall
a night when a soprano was doing her act. She was not in very good
voice — possibly she had a cold. When she got to her second number I saw a gentleman in the stalls produce his evening paper and
proceed to read it until the lady's act was finished. I can well
imagine the dreadful effect this had on the unfortunate soprano.

Indeed, if I have a criticism of Empire audiences, I would say it
was the other way round in its latter days, when American acts
appeared with monotonous regularity. They all received what
I can only call mindless applause. I must be fair and alter that

statement to, every American act I saw got that sort of reception.

Laurel and Hardy, for example, were at the end of their tether but possibly their reception was an expression of sympathy. Jerry Colonna, whose only attribute turned out to be his loud voice, had a rapturous response from the Empire audience. It was more muted for Sophie Tucker, who had seen better days, but even then the night I was there a gentleman in the front row of the stalls stood up as she took her curtain and threw a bouquet of flowers on to the stage. Maybe he had once accepted her invitation to come up and see her some time.

I have, of course, been describing shows at the last of the Empires. I was fortunate enough to see the old Empire, a smaller and more attractive theatre. It had started as the Gaiety Theatre in 1874 and the name was changed to the Empire when new owners took over. I first went there with my father, 69 years ago. I had taken up conjuring as a hobby and, having read all I could about the art, decided that the greatest magician in the world must be David Devant. The Empire, incidentally, seemed to specialise in conjurers and I should think every top performer in Britain, from the Continent and some top men from the United States, including the great Chung Ling Soo, appeared there.

Not that Chung Ling Soo was American, or even Chinese. He was a Scotsman named Robertson who had emigrated from Aberdeen to the USA. He was tall, not to say majestic, and during his entire act he never uttered a word, which was perhaps just as well. He was killed on the stage when performing his famous trick of having a marked bullet fired at him and catching it between his teeth. To this day nobody knows whether it was an accident, murder or suicide. Unfortunately I didn't see him when he was at the Empire, partly because I had given up conjuring by that time.

No, my man was David Devant, though I must admit that, when I saw him on the Empire stage, I hadn't realised how old he had become. When he performed some sleight-of-hand tricks I could see from my seat in one of the front rows of the stalls that his hands were trembling.

Even so, everything he did was perfect. He did his famous eggs from a hat trick, when he produced a bowler hat, recruited a boy and a girl from the audience to stand on either side of him, and proceeded to take egg after egg from the hat. These he handed to the boy or girl whose arms were so piled up with eggs that they started to drop on the floor and break. (If Paul Daniels were doing this, I'll bet he'd say, 'The yolk's on me!')

121

Devant finished with his great Magic Mirror illusion which would take me too long to describe. You probably wouldn't believe me, anyway.

I saw Florrie Forde at the Empire. It was in pantomime, of course, and in the company were a couple of second comics named Flanagan and Allen. I must confess in all honesty that I don't recollect anything they did. Many years later I told Bud Flanagan this. He just laughed and pointed out that that was their first appearance together and they had never been in pantomime before.

When the Empire advertised that their next week's attraction would be Jack Pleasants I decided to go to see him. I knew that he appeared as a gormless Lancashire lad and that he was a famous comedian, but I can't tell you what his attraction was for me. In the event, however, I didn't see Jack Pleasants. In the programme there was a printed note saying that Mr Pleasants was indisposed and would not be appearing.

In those days music halls like the Empire had an electric sign on either side of the proscenium arch. The acts in the programme were numbered and these signs showed the number of the next turn, because the acts did not always appear in the order shown in the programme. When it came to the time when Jack Pleasants should have appeared the signs lit up with the announcement 'Extra'. That was how I got my first sight of the founders of Glasgow's best known music hall family, the Logans.

The extra turn was called Short and Dalziel. Jack Short was a young musician who had been invalided out of the Army in the previous war when he lost his leg. He was mobile enough on stage with an artificial leg. His wife, May Dalziel, was a larger than life lady — I don't mean in size but in her approach to the audience. She could sing and she was one of the funniest women I have ever seen on the stage.

They appeared in a balcony scene in which Jack on the stage was serenading his lady love above. It was hilarious and I completely forgot my disappointment at the absence of Jack Pleasants. So did the rest of the Empire audience and they gave Short and Dalziel enthusiastic applause. Little did I think that I'd be seeing them off and on for years to come.

When the owners of the Empire decided to knock down the old place and put up a much larger building, I was full of enthusiasm. I didn't realise what we were losing. The new Empire was to be the Glasgow equivalent of the London Palladium. Like everybody else, I welcomed this project, not least because I was asked to write

Short and Dalziel (JIMMY LOGAN)

a booklet about the wonderful new Empire. I wish I'd kept it, but the fact is that I've never kept anything and have to depend now mainly on my memory.

The great new Empire was opened to acclaim. The idea that it was the Palladium of Scotland was reinforced when a new Tommy Trinder revue, destined for the London Palladium, was tried out in Glasgow. Trinder could do no wrong as far as Glasgow audiences were concerned. The show was a spectacular one and for a Scottish audience had the additional attraction in having as the principal male singer the Voice of Scotland, Robert Wilson himself.

In due course the Trinder revue went to London and, after it had been running for some time, I went down on business in London and took the opportunity to see it again. It had been beefed up considerably since the try-out in the Empire but one important thing was missing — nae Robert Wilson! I never found out why, but I do know the singer who was substituted, though all right in his way, was not a patch on Wilson. Incidentally, you can get an idea of Robert Wilson's calibre when I tell you that he was principal tenor of the D'Oyly Carte company for several years and played all the Gilbert and Sullivan heroes.

One unusual show at the Empire was presented by Jack Hylton, who was very popular there when he brought his band to Glasgow. The London Symphony Orchestra had fallen on evil days and was in danger of disintegrating altogether. Jack Hylton came to the rescue and took financial responsibility for a tour of British music halls, one of them being a week at the Empire.

I don't know what happened in the other music halls, but the effect in Glasgow was remarkable. So intrigued was I, that I went to see the first night. Perhaps it was Jack Hylton's name but, whatever it was, the place was packed and, being a Scottish National Orchestra aficianado myself, I could tell that most of the audience were not habituées of St Andrew's Hall (which happily existed then).

Naturally, the programme was on the easy side. The highlight of the evening was Gershwin's 'Rhapsody in Blue', in which the soloist was a well-known lady pianist whose name, unfortunately, I forget. What I do remember, though, was that she wore a different dress for each of her appearances and, for the Gershwin, she naturally wore blue. The Hylton touch went all the way.

Few of the audience could have heard 'Rhapsody in Blue' played by a full-size symphony orchestra. The reception was thunderous. Years later I went to the Empire to see that somewhat individual pianist, Liberace, appear. He was supposed to have a tremendous following, particularly among elderly ladies and was actually booked for three weeks. The supply of elderly ladies in the Glasgow and West of Scotland area must have been overestimated because, apart from the first week, the audiences, while not small, were considerably less than Liberace expected. Maybe he needed a Jack Hylton.

Of the many American stars who appeared at the Empire, I place one high above the rest. She was Lena Horne and I have never seen or heard any singer quite like her. Teeny-boppers, thank God, didn't exist then or, if they did, they didn't bop in the theatres. Lena Horne was listened to with love and, can I say it, with respect.

But while I record my personal appreciation of Miss Horne, I must admit that the American who got the most ecstatic reception in the Empire was Danny Kaye. So much so that Kaye, though he was there for just a week's engagement, became a sort of honorary Glaswegian. He made the statutory visit to Lauder Ha' to see the great man there. And he even appeared at a big football match on the Saturday leading the customary pipe band, wearing a Balmoral bunnet and twirling the drum major's staff. Oh, I forgot to mention that his act was quite good too.

In my opinion the finest American comedian to appear at the Empire was the great Jack Benny. I have never seen such immaculate timing in my life. He was assisted by a trio of gigantic Negresses and, as they galumphed about the stage, all Jack Benny had to do was to look at the audience and lift an eyebrow and the audience roared.

To tell you the truth I got fed up with American acts at the Empire and stopped going to the theatre unless it was in the call of duty. I did meet Bessie Love, the American film star who fell in love with this country and decided to stay in Britain, where she proved to be an excellent actress, but I didn't see her on the Empire stage.

A remarkable friend of mine was George Millar with whom I had worked on the old Citizen. He had a very adventurous career during the Second World War, when he was parachuted into France and joined the French Resistance. After the war he became a successful novelist and had a farm in the South of England. To my surprise I got a 'phone call from him to tell me he was coming up to Glasgow with Bessie Love for her week at the Empire. Miss Love was very keen to see Glasgow by night. Could I take them both on a night trip after she had finished the second house?

I said yes, right away, of course. Then I wondered what on earth I could do with them? There was no night life worth talking about in Glasgow, although we could have visited some dangerous places and got into serious trouble. Then I remembered Barrowland, run by my friend Sam McIver, known as the Barras Prince because he was the son of Maggie McIver, the Barras Queen. I 'phoned Sam and told him about Bessie Love. He said at once that he would fix everything.

And so, that night, I became for the first time in my life a Stage Door Johnnie (or Stage Door Jackie, to be exact). George Millar and I waited for Miss Love in the little vestibule where the stage-door-keeper sat until she appeared, fresh from the night's success. She was small and charming and less like a film star than any film star I had met. George had a taxi waiting and off we went to Barrowland. The time was around 11 o'clock.

I gave my name to one of the bouncers at the entrance and Sam McIver came down from the top floor, where the dancing took place. He was a small, sinister-looking man on official occasions, but he didn't look at all sinister when we were having drinks in his office during one of my visits.

I introduced him and he actually went so far as to compliment Bessie Love on her films, mentioning two by name. Then he asked if we would like to see the ground floor arrangements before we went to the top floor for the Barrowland dancing.

He took us through a side door to the enormous place where, on a Saturday and Sunday, the barrows stood in long rows. There the stall-holders sold almost everything second-hand in the world. You'll get some idea of the variety of goods when I tell you that a Scottish mountaineering expedition to the Himalayas, who had to operate on a shoestring, got almost everything they needed from the barrows.

During week days, however, the place was used as a second-hand car market. Sam McIver led us at once to a huge Rolls Royce. 'This,' he announced, 'was the car used by King George the Fifth when he was ill at Bognor. It's not for sale.' We had some more of Sam's patter which was interesting but not what we'd come for. To get things moving I said, 'Do you have any trouble here?'

Sam said, 'Not here, but plenty up the stairs.' He reached into a hip pocket and produced a long, nasty-looking truncheon. Pointing to some indentations near the top he said, 'These are the teeth of a big Irishman I had to throw out last night.' Miss Love looked suitably impressed.

We left the second-hand cars and took the lift to the top floor. I should explain that Barrowland was the most popular dance hall in Glasgow, which was then the most dancing city in the whole of Britain. It was also known for the high quality of its dancing. The band, believe it or not, were called the Gaybirds.

Sam McIver took us to a little balcony overlooking the dance floor, which was crowded with dancers. 'You'll maybe not believe this,' he said to Bessie Love, 'but most of the men dancing there have got a razor ready in one of their pockets. I'm not saying they're going to use it but you never know what might happen. Would you like to dance?' He looked at George Millar.

George asked Bessie to dance. 'Oh,' said Sam as a parting shot, 'if any of these fellas taps ye on the shoulder, you give up your partner to him and look for somebody else. It's a rule here.'

So they took the floor and I watched with interest. I wondered if Sam was going too far. I had also an idea at the back of my mind that some of those present knew that a famous film star would be there that night. George and Bessie managed about three circuits of the dance floor when George was tapped on the shoulder. He surrendered his partner with good grace and soon he was tapping another chap on the shoulder. They got on fine, and there was not the slightest sign of trouble.

Eventually they decided it was back to the Central Hotel for them. They were both staying there. I felt I had maybe let them down but, as we were walking back to Glasgow Cross to the all-night taxi rank, we came to a tenement close which I recognised. There had been a very good murder there a few years back. So I stopped and told them what had happened, then took them into the close. The walls were running with damp and the only illumination came from a flickering gas lamp, adding an eerie touch of its own. I completed my murder story and said, 'Is that enough for tonight?'

Bessie Love assured me quickly that it was and we walked to the Cross and got our taxi to the Central Hotel. I went home, conscious of a good night's work done. But I wondered next day what Bessie Love would be saying about her experiences to her friends in the Empire Theatre.

One last memory of the Empire before it disappeared forever more. We were alerted that a new English comedian, who had been doing well in the Provinces, was to get his first big chance in the Scottish Palladium, otherwise the Empire. I was asked to meet a top theatre man from London who had come up specially to see how the famous (or infamous) Glasgow audience would treat him.

I met the entrepreneur at the Empire for the first house on Monday. The place was half empty and we sat well back from the stage so that Ken Dodd wouldn't recognise anybody. From the moment Ken dashed on, I was for him. I'd never seen such energy on the stage from any performer except acrobats. He just bashed the audience into laughing.

I felt he was the funniest man I had seen for quite a while and I laughed a lot. The great man from London did not laugh once. At length he delivered wisdom, shaking his head the while. 'He'll never last at that rate,' he said.

Ah, well, we can't all be right. I had a picture taken with Ken 'teeth to teeth', for I have much the same occlusion as Mr Dodd has. The only marked difference is that his front teeth are insured for some enormous sum. Mine are not. In fact, they're not even mine nowadays.

The very last performance in the Empire was on the theatre's ninetieth birthday. The Scottish Federation of Theatrical Unions held a farewell show, which was especially notable for an appearance by Albert Finney and Duncan Macrae as a couple of demolishers. Albert Finney was at the Citizens' Theatre for a spell as director (and occasional actor) because he wanted to get experience in that branch of stage work. He had suggested this himself and, naturally, the Citizens' were delighted to co-operate.

Finney and Macrae were very funny in a macabre sort of way because what they were portraying was all too true. Each had a pick and, at the end of their turn, they attacked the stage in reality, pre-empting the real demolishers who were coming the next day. It was eerie to see the picks being driven into the stage. Indeed, it seemed sacrilege. A lot of people went home thoughtful from the theatre that night.

FOURTEEN

THE WEST END PLAYHOUSE

THE   WEST   END
Playhouse? That's surely not a theatre in Glasgow? Aha, I think I
have you got there! The West End Playhouse still stands — lonely
and neglected in a part of Glasgow whose centre has disappeared.
The name on the building is Jimmy Logan's Metropole, when last
seen facing empty spaces in what used to be the bustling St
George's Cross.

If ever a theatre had a hit and miss life it's this one. Harry
McKelvie of the Royal Princess's in the Gorbals opened it in 1913.
Possibly this was an effort of his to establish a theatre on the fringe
of the West End of Glasgow and complement his Princess's on the
other side of the Clyde. Glasgow was moving West in a big way and
it must have seemed a good idea at the time. Why go into the
centre of the city to see a show when you could stop half way at the
West End Playhouse?

That shrewd man, Harry McKelvie, soon found that he was
wrong. He closed the West End Playhouse and put it up for sale
after a mere matter of months. A new company ran it as the
Empress Variety and Picture Playhouse, and the injection of
films,which were new then, kept it going for some years.

Its next metamorphosis was in 1933 when it was bought by
George Urie Scott, who already owned the Pavilion. George Urie
Scott had a wonderful reputation for watching the bawbees — the
tales of his thrifty ways are legion. He renamed it the New Empress
and ran it until 1960, interrupted only by a fire in 1956.

The next owners, for two years, were the Falcon Trust, a group

Renee Houston in her early days, when she did a comic/singing
act with her sister, Billie. They appeared with Tommy Lorne
at the Pavilion, and had great success, too, at the
London Palladium. When Billie left the act to get married,
Renee followed suit but stayed on the stage in partnership
with her husband, Donald Stewart. He died very suddenly,
after which Renee became a 'straight' actress,
appearing on the London stage and in many films.
(SCOTTISH THEATRE ARCHIVES)

of idealists who brought some unusual plays and shows to Glasgow. Then the old Metropole (which had been the famous Scotia Music Hall) was burned down and, though its owner, Alex Frutin, wanted to rebuild it, it was discovered that the foundations rested on sand, like so many of the places near the River Clyde. The cost of putting in proper foundations was impossibly high. So he bought the New Empress and changed its title to the New Metropole.

Alex's father, Bernard Frutin, had been a wig maker for theatres in Russia until conditions there made it imperative for him to leave the country. He had taken over the Metropole and, after his death, Alex had carried it on. At this time Jimmy Logan was very keen to have his own theatre so Alex Frutin sold it to him. He changed the name to Jimmy Logan's Metropole and had a quite adventurous time running it.

He put on Scottish musical shows, and Scottish plays with such actors as Renee Houston, Alec Finlay, Molly Weir and Clark and Murray in them. It was then that Gracie Clark showed what a fine actress she is as well as a superb comedienne. Every now and then,

Jimmy Logan as 'Johnnie Walker'.
(STEPHENS ORR/SCOTTISH THEATRE ARCHIVES)

however, Jimmy put on a big show to please himself. He mounted one of the best productions of *Rob Roy* that I have ever seen. He played the juicy part of Bailie Nicol Jarvie himself and sang a pleasant song which he had composed himself, 'The Bells of St Mungo'. I am still surprised that it never caught on.

In the big scene, Rob Roy and his men were attacked by the English red-coats who came through the aisles firing at the stage and eventually stormed it. The play had a good run but the cast was so big that it must have been difficult to make much money out of it.

Jimmy Logan even had the audacity to challenge the *Five Past Eight* shows at the Alhambra. He had always felt that they depended too much on big names from England and pointed out that one of the most successful of the Alhambra shows starred Stanley Baxter and himself to the great enjoyment of the lieges. So he put on his own summer show with his old friend, Jack Radcliffe, and his sister Annie Ross. It was a sophisticated revue, especially when Annie Ross was on stage.

A building next door to the Metropole had been bought by Jimmy Logan and he had good ideas for connecting it with the theatre and running a first-class restaurant and a night club there. He was before his time. Today such an idea would be welcomed in Glasgow, where things have improved out of all knowledge. But then the Glasgow magistrates were not for having any of this London carry-on.

Jimmy brought in touring shows to the Metropole but his biggest success was with the London production of *Hair*, which had its customary Wee Free reception as soon as it was announced. The young Glaswegians had a different view and *Hair* ran for many months.

Then the Glasgow authorities decided to 'improve' the St George's Cross area. If you go up there today you will see what a mess they have made of it. About the only bit which a Glaswegian would recognise if he returned from working abroad is the sad face of Jimmy Logan's Metropole.

Some theatres, of course, seem to have a hoodoo wished on them. I would like to be proved wrong but I feel that the Metropole is one.

It's likely that theatrical people might agree with me, for they are nearly as superstitious as East Coast fishermen — and they don't come more superstitious than that. Actors will never mention *Macbeth* by name. They call it 'the Scottish play'. This is because it is supposed to have a hoodoo over it. No actor would ever whistle in a dressing room, for the same reason. Then there is the pantomime with a hoodoo over it — *Sinbad the Sailor*. I've never heard the reason for that, but I've no doubt it's arcane in the extreme.

If I am right about the Metropole's hoodoo, I should think another Glasgow theatre in the same category was the Royalty, which later became the Lyric. It stood at the corner of Sauchiehall Street and Renfield Street, just opposite the famous Poverty Corner. The site is now occupied by the Electricity Board showrooms.

It's rather difficult to discover any details of the chequered history of the Royalty. I knew it as the Lyric, run by the YMCA, but my father-in-law, Robert Bennett Miller, remembered it clearly as the Royalty. Some years before the First World War an English impresario named Alfred Wareing arrived in Glasgow with the intent of establishing a Scottish repertory company. (It's odd how often it's the English who want to develop something Scottish.)

He was surprisingly successful and recruited a good, solid company, most of whom were Scottish actors and actresses. Campbell Gullan was one of them and made a high reputation in Glasgow. Scottish playwrights were encouraged and so emerged J.J. Bell, who had created the lovable character of Wee Macgreegor in the Glasgow evening papers. Wee Macgreegor is well-remembered and the drawing of him by John Hassall is still being reproduced in various ways. It shows him with a tammy, a cheeky face and his hands in the pockets of his perfectly ordinary suit of jacket and shorts. No kiltie stuff for Wee Macgreegor.

Alfred Wareing persuaded J.J. Bell to make a play out of the adventures of his hero. It was a runaway success, comparable only to the amazing run many years later of *The Tintock Cup* at the Citizens' Theatre. You were nobody in Glasgow if you hadn't seen *Wee Macgreegor* at least once. My father-in-law had actually tears of laughter in his eyes as he remembered the show.

All was well with the Royalty and then the First World War broke out in August 1914; that was the end of the Wareing repertory company. Apparently the theatre struggled on and was at one time owned by Howard and Wyndham, who also had the King's and the Theatre Royal, but even they could not make a success of the place. They sold the theatre to the YMCA, who had already bought the building next door and were using it as a hostel. The YMCA in those days had a somewhat ambivalent attitude to the theatre. They approved of entertainment, as I knew from the concert parties in their Dennistoun hall, but were worried about their standards. On the other hand, they needed money to help carry on the benevolent work which they did.

They used the theatre themselves only occasionally and tended to prefer to let it to amateur dramatic and operatic companies rather than to professional ones. In fact, the Lyric became largely a home for the amateur theatre in Glasgow, along with the little Athenaeum Theatre in Buchanan Street, which is now the theatre for the Royal Scottish Academy of Music and Drama.

Both these theatres housed the Scottish Community Drama Festival, the Athenaeum for the minor shows and the Lyric for the bigger ones, including Area and Scottish Finals. The SCDA was very big and successful then and a Glasgow Drama Festival alone sometimes lasted for two weeks, because there were so many entries.

I knew the Athenaeum well because I produced pantomimes for the 37th Glasgow (Regent Place UF Church of Scotland) Troop of Boy Scouts there. We were actually able to run for three nights and made a lot of money for the Scout funds.

Our kirk dramatic company, which we called the Regent Players, entered for the Drama Festival regularly. I recall particularly a play entitled *The Lascar* in which I took the title role. It was set in the Captain's cabin of a passenger liner and our producer arranged the set. She excelled herself by using a large table on castors for the Captain's desk. The adjudicator, summing up, naturally reflected on what would have happened to this table at sea.

That was only one of the troubles. As the Lascar, I had to enter the cabin and hold up the Captain and a group of guests aboard the liner until something made my attention wander and a brave young man jumped me and wrestled with me for possession of my revolver. It was that kind of play. Naturally, as is the way of amateurs, I never used make-up at rehearsals and my struggle with my brother George (the hero) went well, including the firing of the revolver.

On the night we were to appear I lavished a dark-brown make-up on my fair white body and congratulated myself on really looking the part. I made my dramatic entrance and all went well until the struggle with the hero started. I was clutching my revolver in my grease-painted hand and, when it came to the time for the shot, I couldn't fire the trigger because my finger was so slippy.

My brother was, of course, dressed in immaculate white flannels and, as we struggled, I suddenly became conscious of the fact that my make-up was coming off on his trousers. He was muttering 'Fire, for God's sake fire.' And at last, by a superhuman effort, I got the gun to fire. I don't recollect how the play ended (or maybe I don't want to) but we were somewhat less than successful in that Festival. Not, mind you, that we were successful in any Festival. The best we ever did was to come 16th out of an entry of 32 plays.

We never appeared at the Lyric because we never got past the first round. But I was there frequently as a critic because I wrote a weekly column under the name of 'Jingle' and attended amateur shows several times a week during the season. It was a hard life.

The show at the Lyric I never missed was the annual *College Pudding* put on by the students of Glasgow University. It ran for a week and was packed out every night. I thought it was tremendously funny, although there were times when I wondered what the YMCA thought about some of the jokes.

I wrote a revue which was put on at the Lyric in aid of the Red Cross. I don't remember the details but I do recollect that it finished up with the biggest chorus line that had ever been seen in a Glasgow theatre. The producer had arranged that the Red Cross girls would march on to the stage to rousing music and so many girls, all of them beautiful, came on that the place was packed and it was all that the cast of the revue could do to get on and take their bow. The war, of course, was in its very early stages and everyone was very patriotic.

I was delighted with the show until another amateur revue came along at the Lyric. It was written and produced by a BBC chap called Alan Melville, who later did not badly in London. My gas was at a peep because I realised that I had not come near the wit and sophistication of the Melville show. It just proves that amateurs should never tangle with professionals.

Occasionally there were professional shows at the Lyric. I have already mentioned the Moscow Art Theatre company. The Scottish National Players put on many of their productions there, including a number of James Bridie plays. The Curtain Theatre, a semi-professional group, staged several of the Scottish plays by Robert McLellan, an outstanding writer handicapped (in the opinion of some critics) because he wanted to write only in the Lallans. His play, *Jamie the Saxt*, dealing with James VI of Scotland and I of England, has been received with great acclaim. But when it was revived lately, very successfully, the younger members of the cast, though all Scots, had to be instructed in the Lallans, which they could not understand. 'Jamie', incidentally, was the role which brought Duncan Macrae to the attention of the professional theatre.

As time went by, the YMCA ran into financial difficulties over the combined theatre and resident building in Sauchiehall Street. They appealed for help from the many semi-professional and amateur groups which used the theatre regularly. 'Save the Lyric' was the slogan. The amateur operatic and dramatic clubs in Glasgow and district rallied round in a big way. They knew how important the theatre was to them, for the Athenaeum was already proving too small, except for little amateur dramatic clubs.

There was great enthusiasm, especially when it was announced that the Lyric had been saved. The big shows could still go on. But it was not long ere the hoodoo struck. The Lyric was sold to business developers and promptly closed. There was considerable indignation among the people who had used it for so long.

I have no doubt that the YMCA was forced, financially, into this position. I never learned what was happening behind the scenes, to use an appropriate phrase. But it was certainly unfortunate at that particular time. Today the situation is completely different. The amateur groups get the use of the King's Theatre for a month in Spring and a month in Autumn. There are theatres of various sizes in Glasgow, particularly in some of the modern schools and in the two Universities, Glasgow and Strathclyde. Many of the professional shows which once played in the Lyric now appear in the Mitchell Theatre, which is part of the fine Mitchell Library.

There is, for example, a summer show which appeals specially to visitors from America and Canada and is included in many tours arranged from these countries. It is very tartan indeed and immensely successful, being in the line of Larry Marshall's 'Jamie' show in Edinburgh. Indeed, you might say that the life of the 'doon the watter' concert parties is now kept going in Glasgow.

Unfortunately the Mitchell Theatre has one or two disadvantages. It was, of course, designed as part of a library and had to fit in with the library requirements. The result is that the auditorium is one of the most comfortable in Glasgow and the stage a good one, but there is no space for flying scenery so that sets have to be slid in from the street. Secondly, back stage accommodation is perfectly adequate for a play or a show with a small cast but somewhat inadequate for big numbers.

This, mind you, has not stopped enterprising people from putting on some fairly big shows, especially if the cast is young and are accustomed to squeezing together! But I remember when Calum Kennedy was putting on a summer season in the Mitchell and using a broom cupboard as his dressing room.

So far, I'm glad to say, there does not appear to be any sign of a hoodoo over the Mitchell Theatre. Indeed, I would say that there don't seem to be any hoodoos left. But I don't want to tempt fate!

FIFTEEN

LAUGH, CLOWN, LAUGH

THE NEAREST I EVER got to being a Scotch comic was on BBC radio, when I once appeared with my partner, Allan MacKinnon, as a comedy duo called Pollok and Shields and cracked all the oldest gags we knew. But we were not seen, of course, so that doesn't really count. My other ambition was to appear as a clown in a circus and I have achieved that. And, while Allan and I received no offers after our Scotch comic act, the circus people said I'd be welcome to join them any time.

At the moment I am thinking of a wee Glasgow man who achieved as much fame as most of the great Scotch comics. His name was William McAllister but he was known throughout Scotland and a large part of Northern England by the name of Doodles. You can tell how famous he was when I reveal that he was a regular partner of Sir Harry Lauder in the game of golf. He played with Will Fyffe as well. The only reason he did not become a first-class golfer was that he had an unnerving habit of doing circus acts during the round and these did not appeal to those strange people who regard golf as a religion.

For example, he was wont, just for fun, to balance himself on one hand on the edge of the sand-box on the tee and, while his legs stayed up in the air in a typical stance, he would hold out his driver with the other hand and make his first shot. His ball didn't travel far but it fairly put his golfing partners off their own stroke.

Doodles was the chief clown of Henglers' Circus in Sauchiehall Street during the winter season and spent the summer in the same

Doodles the Clown, all 4′ 10″ of him, with his daughters
Anna and Betti, 1934. (GLASGOW HERALD)

position in the Blackpool Tower Circus. I'm sorry. I shouldn't have said Henglers' Circus. The original Hengler Brothers were French and they always called the Sauchiehall Street place Henglers' Grand Cirque. Part of it is still there, built into a cinema.

It was a completely traditional circus except for one thing — the Great Water Spectacle which followed the circus acts. Henglers' engaged the finest acts from all over Europe. Their ringmaster was a striking figure, tall, immaculate, with a fine moustache and of one of the oldest of circus families, the Cookes. The duel of wits between the tall Mr Cooke and the very small Doodles went on all through the evening.

Doodles was not really a Clown. He was an August. By tradition the Clown is the elegant chap who wears the cone-shaped hat, the white make-up and the spangled costume. The August is the tramp-like figure who shambles alongside and provides the laughs. On Henglers' posters Doodles and his partner appeared as Doodles and August, but they were really a couple of Augusts, except that Doodles did wear white make-up and a red nose.

We are quite accustomed to the Augusts taking over the act. Grock, of course, was an August and today Oleg Popov of the Moscow State Circus is an August. The funny men of the circus are tramps to the core. There is a tradition that top circus clowns should be able to do practically anything which any other act does, though of course he makes fun of it. Doodles was an acrobat, he was an equestrian, he could juggle, he could even walk the tightrope. He was the uncrowned King of Henglers' Grand Cirque.

In school there were two great subjects of conversation in the winter time. One was the pantomime, but there were so many of these that it was difficult to have a really good argument. There was only one Henglers' Circus and you were nobody if you hadn't seen it. My father had a habit of taking the family to the pantomime first and we didn't go to the circus until some time after the New Year.

You were nobody in your class pecking order unless you'd been to the circus. One day a heated argument arose in the playground about the great Water Spectacle which concluded the show. Apparently there was a scene when the Indians (it was nearly always a play about Cowboys and Indians) attacked a small group of Cowboys on a high hill by climbing up to get at them. The subject of debate was whether the Indians went up ladders or whether they climbed a staircase. Henglers' used the full height of the circus for their scenic effects.

A rare photograph of Doodles out of uniform —
William McAllister with Sir Harry Lauder in 1926.
Sir Harry appears to be checking his scorecard —
or could it be the bill? (GLASGOW HERALD)

I had been asked if I had been to the circus and, not wanting to
reveal my family shame, I said I had. So I was asked which I voted
for — ladders or staircase. I took the side of the leader of the ladder
group because he was a pal of mine and plumped for ladders. And
then, when my father did get around to taking us to Henglers', I
saw that the Indians went up a staircase. There were no ladders to
be seen. But, of course, I couldn't possible renege on my pal. I had
told a lie and had to live with it. That hasn't stopped me telling lies
since then, but I've always regretted them.

On New Year's Day Henglers' gave four performances. One
January 1st, when my second brother and I were old enough to go

such places by ourselves, we went to the first performance at 10 a.m. I had calculated that there would be seats in the gallery at that time of day. We couldn't afford to book seats and the gallery was unbookable. Even at that early hour Doodles was funny and, as far as I could see, we got the whole show. But I couldn't help wondering what sort of condition the performers would be in when the fourth show had been given.

It was the Great Water Spectacle that made Henglers' different from any other circus I've ever seen, and I've seen circuses in Russia, Mexico, New York and Italy. After the last circus act the ring would be cleared and that was when Doodles would make his final appearance. If carpets were being rolled up, you could depend on it that somehow or other Doodles would get rolled up in one and be carried off shouting for help.

Then the circus ring slowly descended and, when it reached a certain depth, water came flooding into what had been the ring. This meant that the audience were now facing a good sized lake. The curtain at the back parted on the scenery, or part of it, depending on how the plot was going to go. As I've said, there was a tendency to go for Cowboys and Indians and on those occasions Henglers' would advertise that rifle shots would sound no louder than the crack of a whip. This was to appease parents who were bringing small children and didn't want them frightened. All I can say is that Henglers' estimation of the sound of a crack of a whip was much louder than mine. But they were the experts and, as I had no small children, I didn't worry.

I was disappointed one year when the water spectacle revolved round a transpontine drama with the heroine being attacked by the villain and tied to a rock in the water so that she would be drowned when the tide came in. Waves started to come in and the heroine was in a parlous plight. Could nothing save her? Yes! Suddenly on a rock at the back of the now turbulent lake the hero appeared, dived in, untied the girl and swam with her to safety. It was not bad, but it didn't come up to Cowboys and Indians.

The one I remember best had a wonderful closing scene. The villainous rancher had pursued the cowboy hero and heroine to the top of a mountain. For some reason the rancher had a gun and the cowboy appeared to have forgotten his. He was demanding that the cowboy should hand over his girl friend so that the rancher could pursue whatever frightful course he planned with the girl.

Just as the drama reached its height something even more dramatic happened. A thunderbolt hit the top of the mountain and clove it in twain. The villainous rancher went to one side and the hero and heroine to the other. Then a great gush of water appeared through the cleavage (there had been, apparently, a lake on the other side of the mountain) and a huge waterfall dashed down into the lake below. Suddenly an Indian in a canoe appeared and shot the falls. He was followed by a whole tribe of Indians shooting the falls in quick succession. The End.

No one in the audience bothered to work out what this scene actually meant. They had seen the Water Spectacle to end all Water Spectacles. When I see some of the rather puny effects at spectacle that I've seen since, I think of Henglers' and am smugly satisfied that I've seen the best.

When Henglers' closed it was rented as a theatre and housed all sorts of entertainments. Its finest theatrical hours were in the years when the distinguished producer, Parry Gunn, presented Glasgow University student productions of *Julius Caesar* and other plays that could be mounted in such a great arena. The scene in which Mark Antony addresses his friends, Romans, and countrymen had a mob so big that no professional production could have matched it. Maybe the acting of the principals was not up to professional standard, but the audience were once again seeing a spectacle in Henglers'.

Graham Moffat brought his *Bunty Pulls the Strings* company to Henglers' but the auditorium was rather large for this type of play. Another impresario tried a music hall show but again the size of the place seemed to intimidate audiences. Eventually Henglers', which had now undergone a series of different names under successive entrepreneurs, gave up the ghost.

When the Circus closed Glasgow Town Council realised that something important had gone out of the city's life, so they resolved to have a circus of their own. They had a fine exhibition centre in the Kelvin Hall, farther along to the West in Sauchiehall Street. So was started what was then the first civic circus in the world and the manager of the Kelvin Hall and one of the Bailies had a fine time touring Europe and America to see and engage circus acts. They made a good job of it and the standard of the Kelvin Hall Circus was well up to that of Henglers' except, of course, for the Water Spectacle, which would have caused enormous construction problems to be fitted into a building which was used all year in the same way as London's Olympia.

There was no Doodles at the Kelvin Hall Circus. I never discovered what happened to him after Henglers' closed. The Kelvin Hall had more clowns, but nobody up to the Doodles' standard. Years later when he was living in poverty in Glasgow the name Doodles had been forgotten and he was plain William McAllister. His death was eventually reported in a Glasgow newspaper. A small paragraph at the foot of a column announced that William McAllister, formerly Doodles the Clown, had been found dead in his lodgings. All he had was £4 and a few of his circus props. That is why I headed this chapter, 'Laugh, Clown, Laugh!'

Once, in search of a story for my newspaper, I spent all night in the Kelvin Hall when the circus, the menagerie and the amusements were all installed. Luckily the manager stayed with me, because it was a most eerie experience. A lion would occasionally roar, an elephant would trumpet and there were queer sounds that could not be identified at all.

Among the side shows was one which had on display two 'man-eating' crocodiles. They were kept in water in a large bath and the elderly owner of the show sat with them, muffled up in coat and scarf. Correction — he sat beside the bath not in it. This was so that he could see that the water for his pets was always kept at the right temperature. Apparently he was quite accustomed to doing without sleep, but I couldn't help thinking it was an odd way to make a living. The crocodiles looked quite comfy, though.

My favourite Kelvin Hall story concerns the football fan who supported Rangers, a club notorious for its clashes with Celtic FC. Most of its followers are of the Protestant persuasion, or claim to be. Celtic is in the directly opposite camp. A goodly proportion of its supporters welcomed the Pope to Glasgow on his recent historic visit.

When the new Exhibition Centre was built in Glasgow and the Kelvin Hall closed until it could be reopened in a new guise, there were Letters to the Editor in the Glasgow newspapers about the Kelvin Hall Circus. The prize winner (at least, in my opinion) was the man who described a dogs' football act at the Circus. It was one of those acts where a team of performing dogs dressed in Rangers' colours 'plays' a team dressed in Celtic jerseys. The writer said that, when the Celtic dogs beat the Rangers dogs, he left the Kelvin Hall and never went back to the circus.

This, to normal persons, may seem remarkable. But I can tell you of a neighbour of mine in Glasgow who was a dedicated 'Blue Nose', as Rangers' supporters are described. He was present at the unforgettable game when Celtic defeated Rangers by seven goals to one. He was so affected by this event that he went straight home to bed and did not surface until four days later. This, to me, is pure theatre.

The Kelvin Hall Circus and Carnival has been transferred to the Scottish Exhibition Centre, now the winter quarters of the Robert Brothers' Circus, and it is no longer a civic affair. As a former circus clown I'm sorry that the old style is not carried on. Not that I ever appeared in a Glasgow controlled circus, but I did make my circus debut in a circus visiting Glasgow, the never-to-be-forgotten Bertram Mills' outfit.

At the time I was writing regular articles for the monthly magazine, Scottish Field. With the publicity man for the Mills' Circus and my Editor, Comyn Webster, I arranged that I should join the famous international clown, Coco, in one of his acts in the Big Top at Bellahouston Park. This was all very well in theory, but the outcome was altogether different. First of all, Coco was an internationally famous clown and had his reputation to think of. Secondly, I was quite unaware of the acrobatics required in the act.

It was one of the traditional acts and starts off with a wallpaper routine and ends with amazing skids through a water-logged ring. I was summoned to rehearsal at an early hour in the morning. To a certain extent I was lucky. Coco explained to me that I could never manage the acrobatics so he was going to make a change in the routine. Then he looked at me closely and said, 'You've a perfect face for a clown.' I was delighted.

He took great care with my make-up and eventually announced himself so pleased with it that he intended to register it with some Clowns' sodality which copyrighted your make-up so that nobody else could use it. Alas, it couldn't be done. It was explained that this register was purely for professional clowns and I was an amateur.

Coco then discussed the routines for that afternoon's performance. His son was his partner and as expert as he was. But in the wallpaper routine I was to come on as an assistant. On the back of my dilapidated swallow-tail coat I had the inscription 'Ass. Boss'. I had to put my chin on a table and be constantly deluged with whitewash. This was fairly simple.

But after that, for some reason which escapes me now, a large cake covered with cream was brought into the ring by Coco. At rehearsal he explained to me that the 'cream' was actually shaving soap and that the cake would be pushed into my face. 'I will rush at you with the cake,' he said. 'And people will think I have pushed it into your face. What really happens is that when I get to you with the cake you take it out of my hands, shut your eyes and push the cake into your face. Then blow out so that you don't swallow anything.'

I looked alarmed and also astonished. 'Don't worry,' Coco said. 'The audience will never notice. They will think I have hit you with the cake. Then you run out of the ring with the cake. Remember, if you don't take the cake from me, I have to hit you with the board and it could break your nose.'

We rehearsed and rehearsed and, not for the first time, I realised that I had a dangerous job. But a kind of recklessness gets into the blood on these occasions and all you can say is 'What the hell!'

I was ready long before my appearance that afternoon. My wife and a friend were in the audience and all I could do was hope for the best. At length Coco, his son and I got into the ring and I carried out everything faithfully. I wasn't conscious of any audience response. The whole thing was to get through without making a fool of myself (which is maybe the wrong attitude for a clown).

I was glad when Coco came rushing towards me with the cake. I took it from him, closed my eyes, pushed it into my face, blew out, opened my eyes and dashed from the ring holding the remains of the cake. I got back to our dressing tent and to something approaching normal. Coco came in and said the equivalent of 'Not bad.' Later I met Cyril Mills, son of Bertram, who said, 'We'll offer you a job any time.' I don't think he was serious. Later still I met my wife who said, 'What was wrong? Why weren't you in the show?' In a way, that was the biggest compliment of the lot.

I've been to circuses in many parts of the world but I still prefer those we have in Scotland. Admittedly, the most remarkable act I've ever seen was in the Moscow State Circus when it was celebrating its fiftieth year. State circuses from all over Russia were invited to send their outstanding acts and the one I'll never forget was from a far outlying part of Russia — in the deep South. It consisted of a high wire act in which the wire stretched to the topmost pinnacle of the circus.

Up this wire rode a cyclist with a beautiful girl balanced on his shoulders. As he drove slowly up she sang an aria from an opera. I regret I can't remember which aria it was because I was so absorbed in the performance, but I do recollect that she was a brilliant soprano and that she was accompanied by the Moscow State Circus orchestra, which is of symphony proportions.

On the contrary I was surprised to be disappointed with the show by the Ringling Brothers and Barnum's Three-ring Circus in Madison Square Gardens, New York. The Americans undoubtedly want to do things bigger and better than anyone else but a three-ring circus is a nonsense. The simple fact is that you can't concentrate on any of the acts. You're afraid that you're sticking to one of the rings when something more exciting may be appearing in the others. If there's one way of getting cross-eyed it's going to a three-ring circus. My only real memory of Madison Square Gardens is of the chaps constantly parading the aisles, selling ice cream, balloons, chewing gum — you name it, they sell it.

We had a pleasant alternative to the American style in Bostock's Zoo Hippodrome in New City Road, Glasgow. It was run by Bailie E.H. Bostock, former proprietor of Bostock and Wombwell's Travelling Menagerie. When he decided to spend the remaining days of his life in Glasgow, where his show had always had the biggest reception in Britain, he offered his animals to Glasgow Town Council to form the beginning of a civic zoo. This would have been an excellent idea but, unaccountably, the Council turned it down.

So Mr Bostock started his Zoo Hippodrome, which was a combination of a menagerie with a theatre. In the menagerie he had a lion-taming act which was just as dramatic as anything which appeared on his stage next door. The lion tamer was a tall, grizzled man with the customary waxed moustache. He ended the act by putting his head in the lion's mouth.

I was most impressed by this and the time came when I was misguided enough to go into a lions' cage and get into the act. I was writing a daily column at the time and the trouble is not with the writing but with finding a new idea every day. One day I was sitting in my room wondering what the hell I was going to write for the morrow when Bailie John S. Clarke came in. Bailie Clarke had been an MP, also (although he was English) the President of the Burns Federation, and was now taming lions twice a day in the Oswald Street Zoo. This was housed in a former kirk and was, at one time, the only zoo in Glasgow.

John was a delightful man. One of his pleasant practices was to ask one of the women reporters to put her hand in a pocket of his overcoat and pull out what she found there. The trusting girl would do as she was told and then nearly faint when she found she had a wriggling snake in her hand. The snake was quite harmless, of course. But maybe I am prejudiced in John S. Clarke's favour, for I am very fond of snakes. To me there is nothing quite so pleasant as the feeling of a snake slipping smoothly through your hands. In a Bangkok temple once, I allowed one of the priests to put snakes all over my head and shoulders so that my fellow tourists could take pictures of the occasion. They were very sleepy wee snakes and I was in no danger.

That day, when Bailie Clarke saw me sitting forlornly at my desk he asked me what was wrong. I explained I had no subject for next day. 'That's all right,' he said. 'Why don't you come into the lions' cage with me this afternoon?' I couldn't think of any reason why I should refuse, so I accepted the kind invitation. 'I'll be on at three,' he said, 'so you come down to Oswald Street about a quarter to.'

He left my office and I started to think what I had let myself in for. I understood that the basis for the John S. Clarke lion taming act was a couple of young lionesses. They had been originally trained by a sub-editor on the Glasgow Evening News, Eddie Campbell, who was very interested in zoos. I recollected seeing a photograph of Eddie with them as cubs. They were about the size of a dog and looked rather cuddly. I felt things might not be difficult that afternoon.

At a quarter to three I entered the kirk and found there was already an audience of about forty people who had paid thruppence each to get in. They didn't know they were going to see me, of course. If they had, they might well have asked for their money back. Then I saw the lions. There was an enormous black-maned male called, I learned, Rajah. There were the two lionesses, Nouri and Delia. They were no longer small and cuddly. They were big and, though not quite as fierce looking as Rajah, quite fierce enough for my tastes.

John S. Clarke entered, bright with enthusiasm. He told me the names of the lion and lionesses, then said, 'Oh, by the way, there's one thing I should have told you, Jack. One of the lionesses, Nouri, is in heat. That means I can't take you into the cage with Rajah, because he would treat you as a rival.' I could only come to the conclusion that Glasgow Bailies were immune from this kind of confrontation. I was also coming to the conclusion that I had made a big mistake in agreeing to find a column in a cage.

'What I'll do,' said John, 'is go in first of all and take the steam out of them. Then I'll put Rajah in a separate cage at the back, where he can't see you, and you come in with the lionesses.'

So the Bailie went into the cage, armed with a small whip made of parachute silk! As a matter of fact, it was lying on the floor of the cage most of the time. Right away he had the three animals bounding around to his commands, though they didn't sound so much like commands as suggestions. Anyway, they did what they were told and the climax came when John S. Clarke took a large piece of raw meat in his mouth and the lion Rajah put its front paws on the Bailie's shoulders and ate the meat from his mouth. I have never seen any lion tamer do anything like that.

John then thanked Rajah and ushered the lion through to the realms beyond. He then got the two lionesses standing facing the audience with their front paws on little stands. I was waiting for the summons and I'd prefer not to describe what I was feeling like. I had kept my coat on, not only because it was a wintry afternoon but I always thought it might afford some protection if a lioness took a swipe at me.

'Take your coat off,' was John's first instruction. I took it off and, feeling naked, walked up the steps to the cage. Those of you who have been in lions' cages will know that you go first of all into a small cage beside the big one. Then the outer door is closed and you are admitted into the cage with the animals.

From outside the cage had looked quite big. Now I realised that it was really small and, with two lionesses, John Clarke and me in it, it seemed to be packed. John said, 'I'll introduce you first of all.' He took me up to the nearest lioness and said, 'Delia, this is a friend of mine, Jack House. He's very fond of lions and I want you to like him.' Then he said to me, 'Pat her on the head.' I put out my hand and gave her head a small pat. 'That's no good,' said John. 'She'll never feel it. Give her a good hard thump.' I patted her slightly harder on the head and she didn't seem to worry.

The Bailie then took me round to the other lioness. 'Nouri,' he said, 'this is friend of mine, Jack House, He's very fond of lions and I want you to like him.' Then to me, 'Pat her on the head.' I put my hand out, again tentatively and Nouri turned her head and growled nastily. 'Don't bother to pat her,' said John. 'She's not herself.' She was the one in heat.

Then the tamer started the lionesses doing fairly simple tricks. What was worrying me was that I had read somewhere that the reason a wild animal attacks is because the human emanates an odour of fear. I was acutely conscious of the fact that all kinds of odours were emanating from me. Added to which, if she wasn't doing a trick, Nouri always seemed to be circling round towards me.

After what I estimated later to amount to eight or nine minutes

Bailie John S. Clarke, lion tamer! (MITCHELL LIBRARY, GLASGOW)

John S. Clarke said, 'Is that enough, Jack?' I assured him fervently that it was and he let me out of the cage. I went back to the newspaper office and typed my story. It duly appeared next day. And the day after that I got the usual anonymous notes and postcards, each saying something in the order of, 'Ha, ha! Tell us another. You never done that.'

Indeed, when next I met John S. Clarke, I told him I wished I'd arranged for a photographer to be present so as to prove I had actually been in the cage with Nouri and Delia. He shook his head. 'That would have been dangerous,' he said. 'I doubt if I'd have been able to control them if there were flashes going off.'

You'd have thought, that as far as animals were concerned, I would feel as if I'd done my bit. But no. The Glasgow Zoo at Calderpark had not long started and was still very much a make-do and mend affair. I got the great idea that I'd like to wash an elephant, so out I went to Calderpark.

But when I confronted Director-Secretary Sidney H. Benson in his nice, new office, he said to me, 'We can't let you wash our elephant because we never wash her ourselves. We believe in dry-cleaning.' So that's how I came to dry-clean an elephant — well, maybe not a whole elephant but a bit of the brow and a patch on the left-hand side, at any rate.

'You must have noticed,' said the Director-Secretary to me, 'that elephants in zoos usually look a sort of dirty colour, whereas elephants in circuses have a clean silvery colour. Well, we got Freda through a circus man, though she's not a circus elephant, and he told us the secret. Never use water on an elephant. A wire brush and pumice-stone are what you need, and if you'd like to start, come on.'

He collected John Crawford, the Zoo overseer, and we climbed up through the trees to the Elephant House. There we found Freda and her great pal Lachie the camel ('Lachie' is short for Camlachie, after the Glasgow school which had helped the Zoo so much).

The Zoo people thought that Lachie was pining recently. He was looking thin, and kept on pacing restlessly up and down in his paddock. When the elephant arrived, they decided to put Lachie in with her. Lachie had been a different camel ever since. It was obviously company he was craving, for he came from Whipsnade where there are a lot of camels.

Victor Rollands, the elephant keeper, was away for lunch so the cage door was locked and nobody there had the key. We looked at Freda and Lachie through the broadly spaced bars, and then John Crawford said, 'Well, we'll just have to go through the bars.'

He was up on the parapet and through the bars in a twinkling. The Director-Secretary gave me a leg up and I scrambled into the cage. Freda looked at me in an interested way and stopped eating her hay. She waved her trunk towards me, looking like a very large tram-conductress saying, 'Fares, please.' Lachie paid no attention to me at all.

John Crawford slapped Freda in a kindly way and murmured sweet nothings in her ear. 'Elephants,' instructed the Director-Secretary through the bars, 'are very fond of petting.' I patted Freda on her trunk and said, 'How are you, old girl?'

I might have been betrayed into further foolishness, but John Crawford shoved a wire brush and a large lump of pumice-stone into my hands and said, 'There you are. Clean away.'

I wasn't quite sure where to start. When you are faced with a four-year-old elephant, weighing about one and a half tons, and standing nearly six feet high, you find that there's an embarrassment of riches. Eventually I selected Freda's brow and started to brush it vigorously with the wire brush.

A delicate powder arose from her brow. I looked anxiously at Freda, but she seemed to be liking it.

'I can see a difference already,' said the Director-Secretary admiringly.

Then I had a go with the pumice-stone. That seemed to please Freda too. A lovely silver sheen started to come up on her brow. It looked so good that I started on her left side with the wire brush and followed it with the pumice-stone. I felt that, in dry-cleaning an elephant, I was doing something really big at last.

John Crawford gave me some cattle-cake. 'Up, up, up!' he cried to Freda, and she lifted her trunk so that I could put some of the cattle-cake in her huge, slippery, pink mouth.

'That's a new one,' said Mr Benson admiringly. 'I've been away for three days at Troon and she's learned a new trick already. In English, too.'

He was referring to Freda's lifting her trunk at the word 'Up'. Freda (whose original name was something like Lishinov) knows her commands in a Hindustani argot, and Victor Rollands had to learn these words when he took Freda over. It didn't worry him greatly because, before he became an elephant keeper, he was a regular soldier in India for twelve years.

Mr Benson, however, was rather sad that Freda hadn't recognised him immediately he came in. In spite of all that you have heard, elephants have very short memories. (Except for the elephant of Ord-Pinder's Circus, of whom you will hear later.)

'If you want to be an elephant-keeper,' said Mr Benson sternly to me, 'you'll have to see that she doesn't forget her tricks. Every day she must go through them. The secret with an elephant is a combination of strictness and kindness.

'You'll look after her feeding and her straw for the night. She can't stand on cement, so that's why we put in these ship hatches. You'll clean these. Then you'll take her for her daily exercise — very important. And once a month you file her toenails and put Stockholm tar on her feet to prevent them from cracking. Above all, you've got to keep applauding her when she does anything clever. Elephants love flattery.' I gave Freda some more cake, while John Crawford produced a couple of ash walking-sticks which Mr Benson bought from a tobacconist's shop in Glasgow. These sticks are used to keep Freda in order, and also to get her to do her tricks. A slight prod on the ankle and she raises that leg.

Mr Crawford patted her on the ear and she trumpeted triumphantly in a manner that would have put the late Louis Armstrong to shame.

Regretfully I clambered back out of the cage. I must say that Freda was the most charming elephant I have met, and I felt that she would turn out to be one of the best-looking pachyderms in captivity.

Another elephant I didn't so much admire as respect was Jumbo of Ord-Pinder's Royal No 1 Circus. The Pinders were originally a French circus family of some importance, who came to seek their fortune in Britain. I don't know where the Ord came in, but by the time I got to know the circus it had become a very wee one. It was still run by the indomitable Mrs Pinder, the last of the line. I met her when the Pinder Circus was paying its annual visit to Glasgow Green during the Glasgow Fair Holidays.

The Glasgow Green Carnival still goes on and is a very big one, but I regret to say it doesn't run to a circus now. When I knew it first, it had not only Pinder but a big boxing booth and a large assortment of side shows, including the smallest lady in the world, Princess Anita, and the largest rat (no name given). I'd love to be able to say that the shows included a flea circus, so that this chronicle could come full circle, but I never saw one there.

Pinder's No 1 Circus made me wonder what their No 2 would be like. It was more like a large marquee than a big top. It was run almost entirely by the Pinder family with two guest acts. Old Mrs Pinder took the money at the entrance and was in complete control of the business side. She kept the takings under her mattress in her caravan.

The circus programme was run by her son-in-law, who appeared as Koko the Clown and, like Doodles, was multi-talented. He had a little dog act and was so good with animals that he also acted as ringmaster. The animals consisted of dogs, some ponies, a couple of good ring horses and the venerable figure of Jumbo, who looked about as old as Mrs Pinder.

Mrs Pinder's two granddaughters took various parts. They were not only equestriennes but also jugglers and acrobats and what you might call general assistants. A very young female Pinder, daughter of Koko, was being trained as an August. When I saw Pinder's No 1 last, the remainder of the company consisted of a strong man act and a married couple who appeared in cowboy outfits and demonstrated a knife-throwing performance interspersed with such business as the wife holding a lighted cigarette between her lips and her husband putting it out with a whip lash. Then, of course, there was Jumbo presented by Koko and assisted by the girls, the ponies and the dogs to make it look like a big act. All in all, it wasn't a bad wee circus at all.

It followed the penny geggie tradition — that's to say, it kept on giving performances all day as long as Koko could entice a big enough audience into the tent. The Pinder tour was restricted to Scotland and it followed a regular pattern every year, based on local fairs and celebrations. In the country districts the local people knew to a day when to expect the Pinder entrance, always led by Jumbo, pulling the big van which held the tents, the props and sometimes circus people as well. It was followed by the ring horses pulling Mrs Pinder's caravan and the fortune underneath the mattress. Then came the ponies and other caravans. To country people in those days it must have seemed quite the circus parade.

This is where Jumbo's memory came in. The elephant had the whole tour off by heart and did not need any guidance as to where the next destination was. Occasionally the circus had to move by night and the Pinders found no need to supervise Jumbo's steady progress. Koko told me that only once did anything go wrong. They were arriving by dawn's early light in one village and the human beings were getting what sleep they could on the way. Jumbo stopped and they knew they were there.

It was a while before Koko got out to check things. He discovered that they were in the middle of a newly-built small housing estate. The houses had been built on the traditional circus and fair ground since the circus was there last. Jumbo was perfectly right, but nobody had told him either.

One part of the Scottish tour which differed from the rest of the country was the Pinder visit to the Borders. Every town in the Borders has its own Common Riding festival and so the circus moved from one to the other in succession because the festivals were spaced out nicely. This was, of course, to allow the riders of one town to visit others in the vicinity. You've got to be tough to be a Borderer. The Common Riding season is a sort of series of Hogmanays.

Koko explained to me that in one of the principal towns (Hawick, I think it was) there is a special circus performance at the end of the big riding day. After various spiritual celebrations the Lord Cornet, leading horseman for that year's Riding, visits the circus with his attendants. A high proportion of them are Rugger players and the best of Scottish Rugger players are often Border-ers. The point of the visit is that the Lord Cornet has to try to do every trick that the Clown does in one special act. I gathered from Koko that he tried not to make the act too difficult but juggling can present problems if you're seeing double.

Alas, there is no Ord-Pinders' Royal No 1 Circus left — at least, as far as I know; and I have only one elephant story left. You may recall my mention of E.H. Bostock. He had Glasgow's best-known elephant in his Zoo Hippodrome. His name was Roger and he was a great favourite with Glasgow people. Unfortunately he succumbed to the dreaded elephant disease of must and there is no cure for it. Sorrowfully Mr Bostock decided that he must be killed. So he engaged a sure shot rifleman who executed Roger with a single bullet between the eyes.

Mr Bostock engaged a taxidermist who removed Roger's skin, stuffed it and made the elephant as good as new on the surface, except for the one bullet hole on its brow. He was left, of course, with an awful lot of elephant interior. Mr Bostock solved the prob-lem of disposal by having the remains buried in a piece of ground below a gentlemen's lavatory on the banks of the River Kelvin.

When I was standing as the Liberal candidate for the Woodside division of Glasgow (now, approximately speaking, the territory of Roy Jenkins), I was asked at one of the meetings what did I know about Woodside, anyway? The idea persists that I am an East-ender, having been born in Tollcross and brought up in Dennis-toun and Riddrie, but in fact I spent only thirty years of my life in the East, and have had fifty years in the West.

I replied to my heckler that I knew that in the division there was an elephant's grave, and I explained the circumstances and where the grave was, which I was sure was more than he could. Despite this display of trivial knowledge I came only third, but with a respectable total of exactly 5000 votes.

The taxidermist's job on Roger was presented to the Kel-vingrove Art Galleries and was shown in their wild life section, complete with the bullet hole in the brow. It's quite a while since I visited the Art Galleries but Roger was dominating the scene then. I hope he is still there and that visitors realise what an im-portant elephant he was.

And now, unlike Roger, I sign off not with a bang but with a sigh of satisfaction that I have reached

THE END

CURTAIN

W<small>HEN</small> Y<small>OU</small> W<small>RITE</small> A book almost entirely from memory (I did check one or two points) you may well make mistakes: nobody is infallible. I apologise for any mistakes I've made and will be glad to correct these if there is another edition. But my troubles are not only of commission but also of omission. In my initial list of people I wanted to mention, I had more than 140 names. I've managed to include a goodly percentage of them but inevitably I have had to leave a large number out. Will those omitted forgive me? I assure them it was only a matter of space which prevented their inclusion.

I am thinking particularly of some of the comics and acts in the minor theatres of Glasgow and round about. They have given me their own mead of enjoyment. For example, I'll never forget the appearance at the Queen's Theatre of the funniest woman I've ever seen in my life, and that's saying something. But I can't recollect her name, though I do recall being left in a completely helpless condition because I had laughed so much.

I wrote about her at the time but, as I have revealed, I have never kept any files or details of any kind from my writings. In this case my remarks about the lady were read by Fred Ferne, when he was manager of the Alhambra and was looking for talent for his next pantomime. He 'phoned me to say he had been to the Queen's and agreed entirely with what I'd written. 'But,' he said sadly, 'she'd never fit into a pantomime.'

I did want to find a place, too, for the Three Aberdonians, one of the finest acrobatic acts I have ever seen. They were not Aberdonians at all, but Fifers. Joe Corrie met them when he was taking his walks around the loch at Lochgelly. They were unemployed and they spent a lot of their free time practising their turn there. They eventually received the honour of being asked to appear at the Royal Command Variety Performance in London.

But I must cease upon the midnight hour or I'll be writing another book! I'd just like to say thank you to all the wonderful people of the music hall, the theatre, the opera, the ballet and the circus for the infinite pleasure they have given me for more than seventy years.

Index